Acting Out Faith

Christian Theatre Today

Acting Out Faith

Christian Theatre Today

Gordon C. Bennett

CBP Press

St. Louis, Missouri

Library of Congress Cataloging-in-Publication Data
Bennett, Gordon C.
    Acting Out Faith.
      1. Theater—Religious aspects—Christianity.
I. Title.
PN2049.B46   1986   246'.7   86-6141
ISBN 0-8272-0016-1

All scripture quotations, unless otherwise indicated, are from the Revised Standard Version of the Bible, copyrighted 1946, 1952, © 1971, 1973.

Printed in the United States of America.

Contents

"God of The Muses"

*Hymn by Richard M. Jones**

Tune: "God of Grace and God of Glory" (Regent Square)

1. God who paints on life's whole canvas
     Hues of depth and vibrancy;
   Whose creative force is moving
     O'er the sweep of history;
   Grant to us your grace and vision:
     Ears to hear and eyes to see.

2. God who pens life's scripts of passion—
     Words and sentences each day—
   Giving cues for all who listen,
     Roles to live and parts to play;
   Grant that we may live your drama;
     Acting out your Word each day.

3. God who spins the wheel for potting,
     Hovering o'er the shapeless grey;
   Breathing soul into the soulless,
     Forming life from common clay;
   Grant that we may sense your Spirit,
     Breathing life into our day.

4. God who orchestrates life's music—
     Strings, reeds, brass, and tympani—
   Forming sounds from life's vibrations,
     In a cosmic symphony;
   Grant that we may lend our portion
     Through lives lived in harmony.

5. God creates the loom for living,
     Weaving life's yarn endlessly,
   Warp and woof together forming
     One great seamless tapestry;
   Grant that we may find the pattern
     Of our common destiny.

*Written for an Arts Festival at Central Baptist Church, Wayne, PA., October 1985. Used by permission of the author.

Foreword

This book is aimed at three possible audiences. One is that of the typical congregation, where people with little or no theatre experience are gamely mounting plays to entertain, edify, and enlighten. Second, there are the more experienced church and college campus dramatists looking for a challenge. Third, there are the faculty and students in Christian colleges and seminaries who seek an intelligent discussion of the basis for Christian theatre.

In addressing these audiences, I have included diverse materials of a theoretical and practical nature. Those impatient to get to the more practical dimension may want to skip the first three chapters. Indeed, those who are desperate to find out what's happening in Christian theatre today may start with Chapter Four; those who want ideas about finding and staging religious plays may start with Five or Six; and those seeking help in writing their own plays may skip to Nine. But, hopefully, others will not find a modicum of history too unpleasant, and I would hope they find my discussion of the artistic and theological bases for Christian theatre somewhat enlightening. An understanding of our roots may help us act out faith more gratefully and courageously.

One caution: Everyone's work is shaped by his or her biases, and mine are obvious. One is that I have less interest in technical theatre than in writing, directing, and acting plays. The lean theatre, what Lope de Vega in the sixteenth century referred to as "three boards and a passion," and what Grotowski calls his "poor theatre," that which relies most heavily on the communicative skills of the actor, seems especially practical for the church setting. So we shall give just brief attention to makeup, somewhat more to scenery and lighting, and much more to costuming—since the latter is something we can hardly do without. Anything an actor wears becomes a costume.

I have another bias, toward plays of substance. Church groups often put on comedies and melodramas just for fun, and that is fine; but here I want to focus on heavier stuff—which is not to discount the role of humor in Christian theatre—but to emphasize a profound drama with a spiritual message. As Christians we should look for a significant drama, emphasizing quality in both the material and its presentation, remembering Elton Trueblood's warning that "holy shoddy is still shoddy." Particularly in light of the slick stuff presented in the media these days, we have to insist that our Christian theatre be done well. The day of "Pray for us, we haven't had time to rehearse," is over. We may be using relatively untrained people, working in limited stage space, with few of the resources available to the professionals, but what we have we use, and what we do we must do well.

My excuse for writing this book is that the previous works in the field are outdated. I've included some topics in *Acting Out Faith* that haven't been treated much in previous works on religious drama: readers' theatre and street theatre, for example, as well as playwrighting. I have had to exclude, unhappily, a detailed discussion of puppetry and clowning, although these are becoming popular ministries. Be aware that plays mentioned in the text are listed in Resources at the end of the book, with publishers' addresses given in "Useful Sources of Materials."

Don't be put off by the *theatre* in my title. There are still people for whom *Christian theatre* is a contradiction in terms, but the word theatre comes from the Greek, meaning a *seeing place*. Certainly the Christian theatre we envision ought to enable people to see clearly. "Where there is no vision, the people perish," we've been told (Proverbs 29:18a, KJV). Like other art forms, theatre can improve our vision, it can help us to see ourselves in a new light. Someone said that a good dramatist can help us find our souls—and it can hold the mirror up to our society. That makes it well worth doing, even apart from its power to amuse.

I need to acknowledge those who have taught and inspired me, and who have given me dramatic experience that made this book possible. As a younger man I was moved by the presentations of troupes like the Bishop's Company and the Redlands Trio, and by such teachers as Ada Grace Cralle and Mildred Hahn Enterline. More recently, colleagues such as Melvin White,

Nonna Childress Dalan, George Ralph, and Todd Lewis have bombarded me with ideas and support, largely through correspondence.

I have been privileged to direct and act in plays at the college and seminary level, and to work with Christian friends of the Philadelphia area in The King's Players. Under the kind auspices of our talented director, Mary Fulmer, I was fortunate to have some of my own brainstorms performed in local churches, and so to grow as a Christian playwright.

Also, I want to thank my wonderful wife, Ruth Bennett, for her patience and support. She has resourcefully stitched costumes and searched for elusive props—she even suffered the loss of her dining room suite for a college set!—and she has fought her way through a living room cluttered with lighting equipment waiting for the next performance. But she has remained caring and encouraging.

So let's begin: "Places, everyone!"

1

Church and Theatre: A Troubled Marriage

The church's interest in theatre seems to have exploded within the past thirty years. Witness the increased use of chancel drama and discussion plays in Christian education, inspirational and fun plays given at church suppers, and street theatre for evangelism and social protest. No longer do churches restrict their dramatic offerings to the annual Christmas and Easter pageants. Puppetry is being used to share the gospel with children, readers' theatre with older adults as well, and the clown ministry for all ages.

Quality religious drama is being written and the size of the playlist increases exponentially. During the past thirty years one major new publisher of playscripts has emerged to serve the growing church market, and during that time at least one major denomination has added a full-time drama specialist to its national office. Seminaries and colleges are adding coursework in addition to their performance ministries.

In Chapter Four I will explore the recent developments in professional Christian theatre as well as what's happening with local congregations, colleges, and ecumenical drama ministries. The fact is that lots of Christians are getting into the act. Drama is a powerful medium and the church is using it again, using it for all it's worth—which is considerable. This is good news about an ancient art form, again used to proclaim the Good News.

Now, a brief excursion into our roots.

The Past as Prologue

A million years ago, give or take a few hundred thousand, when our unsophisticated ancestors were foraging for food, learning to live in tribes, playing with fire, and entertaining thoughts of inventing the wheel and flush toilets, life was a desperate battle for survival. It was an ongoing struggle against the darkness and against the cold, against hunger and death; indeed, the world must have seemed cruel, and primitive people had great difficulty *coping*. As Benjamin Hunningher writes in *The Origin of the Theatre*, "Existence, life, could not be thought of in terms of decades; men managed from season to season, periodically renewing their lease on life. That lease was never bestowed mercifully; it had to be extorted with every ounce of force at the primitive's disposal."[1]

Despite all this, there was the impulse to *play*. Mimicry seems innate in human beings; imitation is fun. It was natural that Oog and Voolka would imitate the monkey or the hawk, the wildcat or the squirrel, as well as members of their own species. They enjoyed pretending, mirroring others, aping the antics of tribal eccentrics. Why? For amusement. To please themselves and others. So the first function of theatre—as it must have happened with these earliest impersonators—is to amuse or *entertain*.

But Oog and Voolka were members of a hunter-gatherer tribe, and when the day's hunt ended, Oog returned to Voolka and the others to share his adventures. Showing the carcass to the excited faces around the campfire, Oog pranced like the bear he'd tracked, he reared up and roared to show how fierce the bear was, and then he mimed hurling the spear, the way the bear fell with a heavy thud, and his own elation at the kill. Oog wasn't good with words—language was slow in coming—but he could make his audience understand everything through mime. They laughed and cheered—or at least the men laughed and cheered as the women, already forced into domestic roles, tended fire and prepared the bear meat for roasting.

But their distant cousins were members of an agricultural community. For Moog and Elkvaa, theatre would serve an instrumental function. Gardeners they were, trying to wrest a modicum of food from the earth, without our modern tools or fertilizers. They were totally dependent on the elements: They had to have enough sun and moisture to produce crops. Any drought was a disaster. When drought came they would implore

12

their deities to send rain—the rain or storm gods, or the fertility gods. To trigger a response from the god and bring about the desired result Moog and Elkvaa might strip naked and dance, as some primitive peoples do today, or don special costumes and headdresses. The idea was that you had to change your appearance radically in order to produce a radical change in nature.

So Moog and Elkvaa and their friends developed an elaborate rain dance, with song and instruments. They may have mimed the effects of the rain, hoping to induce it: the plants bursting with energy, throwing out new branches and green leaves, developing fruit or grain; and then the happy clan, eating and drinking and making merry in the wake of the storm. Perhaps the rain dances became fertility dances and then annual rituals celebrating the victory of spring and summer over death and winter. This sort of playing, Hunningher writes, was an attempt "to bring a certain part of the chaotic world under control . . . The community strove by collective rites to approach and dominate the force which ruled nature."[2]

An excellent example of a fertility ritual, also the first recorded case of theatre in the West, comes from ancient Egypt. (We have an account of it written by a participant, Ikhernofret.) As early as the nineteenth century B.C., there was an annual fertility drama enacted at Abydos, considered the most sacred location in Egypt.

The so-called Abydos Passion Play dealt with the death and resurrection of the Egyptian god Osiris, said to be the Son of Geb (the earth) and Nut (the sky). Osiris, married to his sister Isis, became ruler of Egypt after his father; but his brother Seth envied his power and murdered and dismembered Osiris. With the help of her uncle Anubis (who later became the god of embalming), Isis gathered up the pieces of Osiris' body and revived him. But as a condition of the resurrection, Osiris was not permitted to remain on earth, so he went to become king of the underworld. Later Horus, Osiris' son, avenged his father's death by killing Seth and restoring the kingdom.

A ritual play based on this legend was performed even as late as the sixth century B.C.; also, there were nine ritual plays concerning parts of the Horus myth. These plays were generally staged near temples or at some sacred location, with great ceremony and stately acting, strong makeup and masks designed to enlarge the actors' features, and costumes that became traditionally associated with certain roles.

13

In *Religious Drama: Ends and Means*, Harold Ehrensperger suggests that the Osiris myth took on added meaning as it was elaborated over the decades: It was related to the flooding of the Nile, an absolutely critical event for that society. If the annual flood didn't happen the result was starvation:

> The Nile was called Father Osiris, and the land was known as Mother Isis. The annual overflow was the embrace of Mother Isis by her spouse, during which he impregnated her with the life that was to be born during the harvest. The overflow depended upon the melting of the snow in the mountains by the moon, by the sun. The sun was Horus, less powerful than Osiris because the sun could not give life, since he shone in the desert where all was dead, while life bloomed wherever Osiris touched. Therefore they depicted in their great mysteries the death of Osiris at the hands of the demon Drought, his entombment and Mother Isis' waiting for him, Horus searching for his father and restoring him to life by his magic eye, the sun, and the happiness of Egypt as a result."[3]

Scholars disagree as to whether the Abydos drama was a Passion Play; but even if it was only a ceremonial funeral for Osiris, as some maintain, it must have had dramatic elements. And certainly in the Horus plays, if not in the Osiris, we find this primitive human need to placate or control the gods of nature, whose task it was to fertilize and bring life upon the earth. This was a ritual drama which served religious and educational functions: In addition to its instrumental function, it was a communal rite, a means of socializing the young and making them aware of their common heritage.

And so the earliest theatre fulfilled several functions, satisfied several needs: (1) to amuse or entertain, (2) to report or share information, (3) to invoke the help of the gods. These correspond to Stephen Archer's three primary functions of art: to entertain, edify, and exalt.[4] The first two functions target a human audience only; the third targets the divine. The third is a complex religious function, as we've seen: Invoking the gods is related to the celebration of the seasonal cycle and the initiation of the young into the mysteries of myth and society.

As we develop a Christian theatre worthy of the name we need to keep both audiences in mind. We tend to be much more aware of the *human* heads bobbing out there beyond the stage;

but *we are performing before God as well*, and we do our plays for his sake as well as our own—and we honor him by performing well.

Theatre and the Hebrews

Unlike the Egyptians and Greeks and some early Eastern civilizations, the Hebrews made little use of drama. Indeed, they dabbled very little in art since they were forbidden by Exodus 20:4 to make "any likeness of anything that is in heaven above, or that it is in the earth beneath, or that is in the water under the earth." There were dramatic elements in their religious observances, particularly the annual act of atonement when a goat (foreshadowing, for us, the sacrifice of Christ) was symbolically laden with the sins of the people and sent into the wilderness; but there was no theatre as we know it today. But the Hebrews came close to some genuine theatre with the acts of the prophets, and with the dramatic literature of the book of Job.

Over and over God sent the prophets forth with a single, simple message: "Shape up or ship out! Repent or perish!" God knew that you had to dramatize a message to get people's attention so, for example, he told Isaiah to go about naked and barefoot for three years (we blush to say), as a sign that Assyria would conquer Egypt and Ethiopia; and so it made no sense for the Hebrews to make defensive alliances with those nations (Isaiah 20). And Jeremiah was told to walk around with a yoke on his neck (Jeremiah 27) as a warning that God was going to support Nebuchadnezzar, King of Babylon, who would be his agent in history. In another incident, Hananiah, the prophet from Gibeon, "took the yoke-bars from the neck of Jeremiah the prophet, and broke them" (Jeremiah 28:10). But Jeremiah disagreed with Hananiah's good-news message: Hananiah was a false prophet, and he died that same year.

We find a more detailed dramatic event in Ezekiel:

And you, O son of man, take a brick and lay it before you, and portray upon it a city, even Jerusalem; and put siegeworks against it, and build a siege wall against it, and cast up a mound against it; set camps also against it, and plant battering rams against it round about. And take an iron plate, and place it as an iron wall between you and the city; and set your face toward it, and let it be in a state of siege, and press the siege against it. This is a sign for the house of Israel. (Ezekiel 4:1-3)

15

This was a simple drama. Assuming the "brick" was a large one—perhaps a piece of slate—Ezekiel's sketch became the backdrop for a play in which God warned everyone that Jerusalem would be attacked. Indeed, Dr. Herbert G. May suggests in his *Interpreter's Bible* exegesis that such pictures of Palestinian cities under siege may be found today in the artifacts unearthed by archaeology.[5] Here the dramatic action consisted of Ezekiel's lying bound on his left side for 390 days to symbolize the years that Israel would be punished, and forty days on his right side to symbolize the punishment of Judah (Ezekiel 4:4-8), and to eat unclean food to show that the Israelites will have to eat unclean food when that grim day comes (Ezekiel 4:12-15). Considering both left and right-sided performances, Ezekiel's play would have had a very long run!

Dr. May cites additional dramatic actions: during the reign of Solomon, Ahijah tore his clothing into twelve pieces and gave ten to Jereboam, demonstrating how God would divide Solomon's kingdom (I Kings 11:29ff); and Zedekiah made himself horns of iron symbolizing the defeat of the Syrians (I Kings 22:11).

The Book of Job

Moving to wisdom literature, consider *Job*. The Prologue and Epilogue are in prose and the rest in verse. Our hero, a righteous man of great faith and integrity, loves his family and is loved by them. But when God calls Satan's attention to this "blameless and upright man, who fears God and turns away from evil" (Job 1:8), Satan argues that if Job's prosperity were taken away he would deny God. God therefore gives Satan the right to test Job and the result is an experiment in faith and courage.

Satan strips Job of all his possessions, even his children, and then afflicts Job with disease. But despite his wife's bitterness Job continues to maintain faith in God. Three friends come by—later a fourth—to offer sympathy, but they turn out to be poor "comforters"—indeed, they end up scolding Job. They believe in the age-old principle that doing good brings good and doing evil brings evil, so Job must have done something wrong: He should repent and confess his guilt. Job denies all this but finally, when he hears the voice of God in the storm—and when the Almighty cites his accomplishments, the profundities of the divine wisdom etc.—Job is forced to admit his own smallness and promises to say no more.

In an Epilogue, God rebukes Job's friends for speaking lies and he restores Job's fortune and provides him with a new family. We read that Job has many descendants and lived to a ripe old age.

Job is dramatic literature. There is no evidence that it was ever performed, although it bears resemblance to classical drama. Theodore of Mopsuestia in the fourth century thought it was modeled on Greek plays, and in this century, H. M. Kallen contended that the book takes the form of Greek tragedy, including the chorus and the *deus ex machina* conclusion.[6]

Literally, *deus ex machina* means "God from a machine," and refers to the ancient Greek method of resolving the plot by dropping a divine figure from above to the stage below. Now the phrase is often attached to any play with a manipulated or unconvincing ending. In *Job*, God's answering Job from the storm compels Job's remorse and brings about the denouement. The divine speech is convincing as a reaffirmation of the divine power and mystery, but it doesn't solve the problem of evil.

Modern dramatists have caught the dramatic potential of *Job*. Albert Johnson wrote a one-act version, *Whirlwind*, for his Drama Trios in the fifties. Two major playwrights have created full-length treatments: Neil Simon's *God's Favorite* is amusing but lacks the depth and wisdom in Archibald MacLeish's *J.B.*.

MacLeish's *J.B.* is set in a circus tent, after the show is over and the lights are dim: There are canvas and naked bulbs, and costumes draped about, and poles, ladders, platforms. Two old circus venders wander in: Mr. Zuss (transparently Zeus, the ancient Greek deity) and Nickles (Old Nick) who, it turns out, is to play Satan. They don huge masks and intone the lines of the Bible Prologue, establishing the story.

After the Prologue the play consists of seven scenes. The first establishes "J.B." as a prosperous New England executive. We see him with his happy family, sitting at the dinner table. Here J.B. insists that the affluence and ease represented by their Thanksgiving feast is not anything they've earned but is a free gift of God; Sarah, his wife, thinks otherwise, but her fears and doubts are drowned in the gaiety of the occasion and J.B.'s irrepressible good spirits. MacLeish then uses several scenes to describe the calamities that befall the family: They come pounding J.B. like successive breakers on a beach. MacLeish brings us face to face with our own suffering and the evil in our modern world: We are struck by the callousness and cruelty in the human race, and we know it could happen—*has happened* to us.

MacLeish provides a dim, foreboding scene with J.B.'s comforters, contemporized as a Marxist, a Freudian, and a modern cleric—and, as counterpoint, a Greek chorus of suffering women. Then God's voice is heard, powerful and commanding, and everyone is silent before it—MacLeish falls back on the biblical language at this point.

Indeed, MacLeish's fine verse is studded with refrains from the biblical text. In a *New York Times* essay, MacLeish admitted that he had "constructed a modern play inside the ancient majesty of the book of Job," but he was driven by necessity: "When you are dealing with ideas too large for you which, nevertheless, will not leave you alone, you are obliged to house them somewhere—and an old wall helps."[7]

Unlike Albert Johnson's *Whirlwind*, where the encounter with the Almighty takes place offstage and then Job reports it to his wife, MacLeish involves God more directly. But both Johnson and MacLeish evidently find the biblical ending, with everything turned completely right-side-up, unconvincing. Their endings are less pretentious, but hopeful. *J.B.* ends with the return of Sarah, the reconciliation of husband and wife, and an emphasis on human love as giving power to endure.

Critics differ on the message in *J.B.* Murray Roston, quoting from MacLeish's essay on Job in *Christian Century*, finds that a "primary message of the book is God's need to prove that man can love him for love's own sake. . . ."[8] Or, as MacLeish put it, "Without man's love God does not exist as God, only as creator, and love is the thing no one, not even God himself, can command."[9]

This is a provocative insight. But for Marie Philomene de los Reyes, the theological problem with *J.B.* is the line, referring to God: "He does not love. He is." She believes that this contradicts the biblical truth that God is love. Instead, God is power.[10] And at the end of the play we have no answer to the initial question, "Why does God make us suffer?" Instead, "the play descends to the humanistic plane exalting man for being able, through love, to bear suffering, regardless of its apparent meaninglessness."[11]

Granted—but the play is evidence of MacLeish's faith-struggle and needs to be understood as such. It doubts and probes and questions justice, but *J.B.* is honest and forthright; and to the

18

extent that it helps us deal with the issue of suffering in our lives, the play is worth a good many fine Christian plays of orthodox nature but of little real depth. The Bible speaks to us anew in MacLeish's provocative imagery.

The Troubled Marriage: Five Acts

We've discovered a promising betrothal. Historically, theatre and religion were bound together from the first. The relationship began with primitive man, continued with the dramatic rituals of the Egyptians and Greeks, and reached its early zenith with the great classical dramas of Aeschylus, Sophocles, and Euripides in the fifth century B.C. This was a pre-Christian era, yet it shows how tightly bound religion was to theatre. Greek theatre evolved from the Dionysian revels and rites of spring; and in such noble dramas as *Oedipus Rex* and *Antigone* we find human beings driven by apparently uncontrollable fate, yet determined to know themselves and their destinies.

But the relationship between religion and theatre—later *church* and theatre—has been a difficult, tempestuous one. There are perhaps five acts to this epic marital drama. ACT I, the pre-Christian era of the great Greek theatre, depicts a good strong bond, shows a successful wedding of the two. But then we come to ACT II, and the first separation.

ACT II is set in the Roman era, with the advent of Christianity. Early Christians hated the theatre because of the crude Roman mimes, puppet shows, and farces. Much of the Roman theatre degenerated into spectacles like the gladiatorial shows, where brutality and blood were commonplace. In these events, Christians were often victims and made the objects of ridicule. Church fathers, notably Cyprian, Chrysostom, and Tertullian, thundered against the immorality of the stage, and church councils hurled their anathemas against actors. Consequently, when Christians finally won acceptance in the Empire with the conversion of Constantine, they dealt the theatre a near-fatal blow. It survived only in the East, around Byzantium, and in the attempts of minstrels during the Dark Ages to keep the flame burning.

But there was a reconciliation or remarriage: ACT III is a happy one. The Roman Catholic Church of Medieval times, seeking a way to illustrate doctrinal themes and inform an illiterate congregation about the Bible, hit on drama as a way of

19

educating people and making the faith fun. It got to be too much fun, perhaps, or at least some thought it was becoming too bawdy or secular, so in A.D. 1210 Pope Innocent III threw the players out of the churches—but they continued to perform their mysteries and moral plays outdoors for centuries.

As theatre came under attack from pious conservatives, however, we come to another era of alienation: ACT IV represents a real divorce between church and theatre. We have come to the Puritan period when, in 1642, the English theatres were torn down and theatre was forbidden, then renewed with the restoration of the monarchy in 1660; but, taking the form of ribald and immoral comedies, theatre was again severely criticized.

Even much later, in America, theatre was suspect: In the eighteenth century some colonies and states passed legislation against it, and Quakers, Puritans, and hard-nosed Presbyterians combined to attack it. Today there are still certain fundamentalists and others who discourage attendance at movies or plays; but this is now a minority view, whereas in some periods and places a majority of Christians were opposed to theatre. Today, living in a more enlightened age (regarding theatre), ACT V, there is a new burst of interest. Church and theatre, if not bedfellows, are at least talking to one another.

So we have a five-act epic about a very fickle relationship—with an apparently happy ending. But this is surprising: Why should anyone be opposed to such a benign form of entertainment as theatre?

Pretend that you are judge or jury at a hearing called to examine the question of the legitimacy of theatre. First we'll examine the case made *against* theatre by certain Christians; then the case *for* it. You decide on the merits of the two arguments.

The Case Against Theatre

Theatre was at its worst when Christians discovered it. The popular Roman mimes and farces were licentious and erotic; and there were the brutal spectacles of the coliseum. The church came under persecution and so anything Roman was suspect. So Christians refused to join the Roman army or pay taxes to Rome, or have anything to do with the Roman theatre.

Even when the church embraced theatre later, some dissented. When the mystery and miracle plays were going strong about 1375, an unknown English preacher penned a list of pros and cons for plays, with his longer list being cons. Theatre, he argued . . .

> (1) Played not to the worship of God but to the approval of the world. (2) Men are converted by miracle plays just as evil can be the cause of good, i.e., Adam's evil caused Christ's coming. More people are perverted than converted. Plays are condemned by Scripture. (3) Men weep, not for their own sins, nor for their inward faith, but for their outward sight . . . . (4) Conversion is an act of God. . . . The truly converted will hate such playgoing. (5) Recreation should consist of doing works of mercy for one's neighbors, not in false vanity. Wicked deeds of actors and spectators prove plays' worthlessness. (6) Painting, provided it is true, Christian and restrained, may be a book to discover truth. But acting is an appeal to senses. Good men, seeing that time is already short, will not want to spend it in playgoing.

Our second witness for the prosecution lived during the English Restoration, after the Cromwellian Puritans ruled the country: Now the monarchy was restored under Charles II and the theatres were doing comedies which seemed to celebrate promiscuous relationships and adultery. Our witness, Jeremy Collier, was a clergyman who in 1698 published *A Short View of the Immorality and Profaneness of the English Stage, Together with the Sense of Antiquity upon this Argument.*[12] In his Introduction Collier describes the topics and vices he intends to cover:

> Their (the stage-poets) Liberties in the Following Particulars are intolerable, viz. Their Smuttiness of Expression; Their Swearing, Profaneness, and Lewd Application of Scripture; Their Abuse of the Clergy; Their making their Top Characters Libertines, and giving them Success in their Debauchery. This Charge, with some other Irregularities, I shall make good against the Stage . . . and First, I shall begin with the Rankness, and Indecency of their Language.

Collier's *Short View* with its long title raised a storm of controversy: By 1725 there were more than forty books and pamphlets about the issues he raised!

Collier argued that literature in general, and plays in particular, evoke strong feelings, such as love, ambition, and honor. These sentiments make the world *seem worthwhile*. But Christianity teaches, he believed, that the world, flesh and devil *are evil*—and so anything that makes the world seem worthwhile has to be evil! This syllogism is similar to the argument advanced at those times when the plague infested London and forced temporary closings of theatres:

> The cause of the plague is sinne
> The cause of sinne is the plays;
> Therefore the cause of the plague is the plays.

Collier thought theatre was a plague and the source of many evils: "On what unhappy times we have fallen! The oracles of truth, the laws of omnipotence, and the fate of souls are laughed at and despised! That the poets should be suffered to play upon the Bible, and Christianity be hooted off the stage!"

Let's take one last witness, this one from our own century. *The Sunday School Times* of December 7, 1947, published an essay, one of four installments by Dr. H. Clay Trumbull, on the topic, "Does the Stage Injure an Actor's Personality?"

Trumbull begins with the claim that medically "the persistent simulation of disease tends to produce the disorder simulated." He argues that an actor who has to assume the character of another person over and over, will become more and more like that person; and if the character is evil, that evil will begin to control the actor. This is the contamination theory, that playing a role requires adoption of its attitudes or behavior: there is a transference from the role to life. Trumbull cites an actor who had committed 15,000 murders on stage, another who had been divorced from 2,800 wives, etc., and he asks, "Can any intelligent person . . . believe for one moment that the deliberate and purposed indulgence in simulated evil to any such extent has had no effect in deadening the moral nature of the actor to the enormity of the offenses simulated, or dallied with?"

But what of an actor who plays both good and bad characters? Trumbull contends that "If a man or woman tries at one time to seem better and at another time to seem worse than his or her real self, the tendency of such acting as a whole must inevitably be toward the lower rather than the higher standard—since it is always easier to go down hill than to go up."

In summary, the main arguments *against* seem to be these: (1) theatre attracts the lower elements of society and displays impure passions and immoral acts on stage; (2) as an appeal to the senses,

22

it glorifies the world, flesh and devil as against the spirit and soul; (3) it corrupts its players because they permit themselves to be used by immoral characters; the contamination of spectators follows, because they share the actor's humanity.

The Case for Theatre

The debate about theatre has by no means been confined to England and America: Consider the debate over *Tartuffe* in seventeenth century Paris. Moliere, a gifted comic playwright under Louis XIV, contrived a witty satire on pretense and false piety which he called by the name of the hypocrite in the play, *Tartuffe*. This character worms his way into the favor of a wealthy merchant, Orgon, by pretending to be deeply religious. His piety impresses Orgon so much that he takes Tartuffe into his house, makes him his private chaplain, in effect, and proceeds to deed his property to this imposter who is not only playing a con game on Orgon but is trying to seduce his wife.

Some thought that Moliere was using a particular clergyman of his day as his model for Tartuffe: The times were not lacking venal clergy. Moliere denied that, but the clergy took the play as a personal affront. The church leaders rallied the Bishop against the play, the Bishop got the king's ear, and for the first time Moliere lost the backing of his patron. Louis XIV ordered the play banned after one performance. Moliere had to be content with private readings of *Tartuffe* for five years until, after a good deal of begging and several rewrites, King Louis permitted its return to the stage in 1669.

Moliere's reply to his critics, in the preface to the new edition of the play, is well-argued. They said that *Tartuffe* held the church and the faith up to ridicule; Moliere argued that he had made it very clear in the play that Tartuffe was a hypocrite, that there is a difference between false and true religion, and that it was only the false he ridiculed. The critics said that the theatre was no place for a discussion of religion; Moliere responded that the theatre had its origin in religion and that even now in Europe, and particularly in Spain, the mysteries were being performed at church festivals. He added that "if the purpose of comedy be to chastise human weakness I see no reason why any class of people should be exempt." Moliere said that theatre "is a great medium of correction" and it can correct the vices of men, who are more

23

likely to be laughed out of their sins than scolded out of them. "People can put up with rebukes but they cannot bear being laughed at: they are prepared to be wicked but they dislike appearing ridiculous."[13]

"I am reproached," he continues, "with having put expressions of piety into the mouth of my impostor. But how was I to avoid it if I wished to present the character of a hypocrite?" How indeed? Moliere has made the case for theatrical realism.

Moliere continues by admitting the obvious, that during some periods of history theatre has been decadent and corrupt. He points out that everything in the world can be turned to evil purposes, but we have to distinguish between the false and true in theatre, as well as in medicine, philosophy, or anything else. He goes on to concede that other places may be more conducive to enlightenment and devotion than the theatre. But, assuming "that intervals in the exercise of devotion are permissible and that people need some relaxation, then I maintain that there is none more harmless than the theatre." Moliere seems to suggest that first, the theatre may seriously attempt to reform society, later that theatre's simply entertainment; both arguments have merit.

But what of that old argument that playing the hypocrite—or the adulterer, the embezzler, or just a snob—will have a strong negative influence on the actor?

Let Dale Rott be our last witness. Professor Rott has considered these issues under the title, "Drama," in *Christ and the Modern Mind*.[14] Rott admits that the question of whether an actor should impersonate an immoral character has bothered some Christians, especially youth. It needs a straight answer. Many would balk at committing the sin of murder or prostitution in real life; why then should they impersonate a murderer or a prostitute on stage? The "abstain from all appearance of evil" rule of 1 Thessalonians 5:22 (KJV) might apply here. But Professor Rott gives three very intelligent answers, which I shall paraphrase and extend.

First, the stage person is not the real person except in a metaphorical sense. When Rodney Jones becomes a murderer on stage, or Mary Smith a prostitute, Rodney and Mary are no longer themselves; they are their characters. They are not pretending to be so-and-so in the play, like a secret agent using a "cover" pretends to be a cabdriver in the sense of claiming to be that person. Rodney and Mary *become* their characters if the audience is willing to suspend its disbelief—but both parties know that it's only for the duration of the play.

Some friends may still see only Rodney and Mary on stage; but if they have any sense of theatre and accept the conventions, and if Rodney and Mary do a competent job of acting (and stay *in character*!) the friends will see the characters, no longer Rodney and Mary. Indeed, Mary's best friend may say later, over coffee, "There was a stranger on stage tonight."

The point is that drama is not reality but a representation of it; and the stage is governed by a set of rules, or conventions. When the play is over the curtain drops, the lights go off, the costumes are shed, and Rodney and Mary don their own apparel and return to "real life," whatever that means—and the audience as well. It is an unfortunate and rare event when spectators confuse stage reality with real life, as did the cowboy-spectator watching an Old West melodrama, who angrily jumped to his feet and shot the villain! That should never happen. And if in general spectators are not fooled into thinking that the Rodney they see in a friend's car after the show is a murderer, neither is Rodney.

In *Time to Act*, Burbridge and Watts remark:

> As far as an actor "becoming like his evil character is concerned, this is not really the danger. What he will discover—on the contrary—is that there are many aspects of his personality and thought-life which identify with the part he is playing but which belong to him and are nothing to do with a fictional creation. In recognizing this evil he needs to surround himself with prayer and forgiveness and use his Christian perspective to give credibility to his acting.[15]

Second, one may argue that the end justifies the means. A play may contain a murder or some reference to prostitution, envy, greed, or drug abuse, but if the total effect is to warn the audience against those dangers, or to present them in a negative light, then this seems to justify Rodney and Mary playing unsavory characters. Indeed, this may be an exception to the rule about ends and means.

Third, there is the question of standards and judgment. Who is to say which behaviors are sinful? Each observer makes his or her own judgment on that score, and if we follow the rule that sins should not be staged we will never have consensus on which acts are sins. Again, the integrity of the play—and its potential impact—has to be considered above its detail: Does it enhance one's reverence for life and for the Creator, and for God's truth?

Does it bring one into a closer relationship with human beings, and the God-in-Christ? Is there a redemptive element?

These issues will be examined later. For now, let us say that anyone deciding whether to audition for a play of questionable impact needs to examine more than just the one character being auditioned. But how do we assess the moral value of the play as a whole? Can we use "artistic realism" to justify the portrayal of sin and vice in our plays? The answer often is yes—but we must be careful. Again, Professor Rott: "If the playwright's dialogue and action aims at sensationalism or gimmickry, then he is committing a spiritual/aesthetic sin; but if he feels the realistic action or word develops character or plot which in turn clarifies the God/man relationship, then it is difficult to criticize the realism."[16]

There are several additional reasons why the church should be using theatre today. Drama is a medium that is being explored and exploited by commercial interests at an expanding rate, particularly as cable television emerges with its many new channels voraciously gobbling material. We need to find ways of using drama, on stage or in movies and television, to present that which is just and beautiful and true about our world and about God, in contrast to the commercial drama (especially the soaps) which often exalt base motives and glamorize evil deeds. Also, there is a powerful theological basis for theatre, as we shall soon see.

In Conclusion . . .

It has been a stormy marriage. Some of the altercations might be called "lover's quarrels," I suppose, for the church has so often returned to theatre, as if theatre were magnetic, as indeed as an art form it is.

Perhaps there cannot be a good or a lasting marriage between unequals. If the church takes a dim view of theatre, or *vice versa*, there can be no real partnership.

Today the church seems to respect theatre as a medium, and seems to be more willing to use theatre than in the past. For its part, theatre often seems uncomfortable with the church, and yet so many modern playwrights seem to be probing human existence, asking the important religious questions; and in shows like *Godspell* and *Jesus Christ Superstar* we feel the natural lure the Bible has for secular as well as Christian authors.

26

And as Dr. M. James Young of Wheaton College has said, as part of an interview printed in *Universitas*, when either theatre or the church are less than what they ought to be, they will have a poor marriage. Theatre was less than its best during the Roman period and later, during the Restoration; and the church was less than its best during the Middle Ages and the heyday of Puritanism. In Professor Young's words, "When the church has been most the church, most the Body of Christ, and when theatre has been most theatre—a questioner and revealer of what it means to be human, then the marriage has been exciting and the union has been close."

We see the union today. But as we Christians write, perform, and watch exciting, inspiring theatre, we need to remember Oog and Voolka, Moog and Elkvaa. The same functions of theatre exist now—to amuse, to educate, to tell a story, or to seek God's help.

Incidentally, one of the first Christian martyrs was an actor. A Roman actor, Genesius, was asked by the Emperor Diocletian to perform parodies ridiculing the new religion, Christianity. It was while Genesius was parodying the Christian rite of baptism, that he had a vision of the Lord Jesus Christ and knew that the one he was mocking was indeed the savior of the world. Henri Gheon, a French Christian playwright, dramatized Genesius' martyrdom in *The Comedian*, where he writes in his Foreword, "The character has taken hold of the actor: The divine grace completes what the drama begins."[17]

Performing does change one's perspective in any case. The actor has to get outside himself or herself and into the mind of another, and to some extent this indwelling occurs in the spectator as well. Viewers are not always affected as much as the student who told me that she became a Christian through watching *Godspell*, but they are, to a degree, influenced. Ideas planted by the play in people's minds may in fact grow by grace and produce changed lives.

If we can find the right vehicle, a play that is theologically and artistically sound, and perform it to the best of our ability, we can leave the result to the Holy Spirit who moves among performers and viewers, opening minds and touching hearts.

2

Art and Theatre:
A Few Digestible Definitions

My student was disturbed and disillusioned. She had been to see a Passion Play at a downtown church. The play was well-produced, indeed captivating. But when she entered the Ladies Room during intermission she found the Virgin Mary lounging there, casually smoking a cigarette and looking very "worldly." My student was put off by the apparent contradiction between the actress and her character. Perhaps a day later she could have seen that person in a bar and it would have meant nothing; but that evening, within the framework of the play, so to speak, to discover that the Virgin Mary was a person with very human vices severely affected this viewer's dramatic appreciation.

This student had made the mistake of confusing the actress with the character; an unfair judgment, for we must not expect any actor to be very much like the character being portrayed, certainly not to remain the character *offstage*. But the incident also illustrates the awesome power of theatre to grip the viewer.

Another story that went around years ago, concerned a woman who attended a performance of *King Lear* in Central Park, New York, on a clear, starry night. At the beginning of Lear's mad scene, which was accompanied by flashes of man-made lightning and claps of timely backstage thunder, the woman was observed to become very anxious. Looking at the sky, she dug into her purse, extracted a folded plastic rain hat, and wore it apprehensively through the rest of the scene.

This story, of course, highlights the show's technical excellence. It also demonstrates that a person can become so immersed in the private world of a play that it becomes, at that moment, her *total* world.

This confusion of the line between art and life is more evident in theatre than in most other arts. An indication of this is the extent to which the stage is commonly used as a metaphor of life. The prime example is Shakespeare's:

> "I hold the world as but a stage, Gratiano—
> A stage, where every man must play a part,
> And mine a sad one."
> —Antonio, *Merchant of Venice*

The metaphor takes form often in our conversations. Discussing people we say things like, "Stop putting on an act!" "Cut out the histrionics!" "Don't be so melodramatic!" "She always has to be in the limelight!" And a cartoonist has a patient complaining to his psychiatrist, "Whenever I get my act together, the curtain comes down!"

Elizabeth Burns, in her book *Theatricality*,[1] points out that children love to play-act, as we all know; and so do mental patients. One patient said of her institutional stay, "I have to pretend every day that I'm here, that I'm gay and happy—in order to stay out of the isolation ward. So I laugh and pretend that I'm gay." A nurse told the relative of a mental patient that the patient was much improved, and as a sign of improvement the patient was playing Scrabble a good deal. The next day that patient confided to someone that she and her friends had recently taken up Scrabble as a means of impressing the staff with their ability to think clearly and to be sociable.

But not only do the mentally disturbed play games: we all do! Psychologist Eric Berne has actually catalogued the interpersonal games that we indulge in to satisfy deep ego-needs.[2] Surely we all wear masks—the Greeks used masks in their theatre, and their word for mask was *persona*, person. As teachers, students, employers, employees, parents, sons, daughters, friends, lovers, we play roles and wear masks and adopt certain behaviors in our roles. One does not talk as severely or joke the same way with one's father as compared to one's best peer-friend, for example; and one may swear at one's peers but probably not at one's boss. We learn how to act and talk according to circumstances, according to the roles we are placed in—no one is actually "himself" or "herself" consistently in all circumstances. Indeed, we may never quite know who the real "self" is. St. Paul seems to authenticate role-playing for a good reason: "I have become all things to all men, that I might by all means save some" (1 Corinthians 9:22).

Evidently role-playing is acceptable if it lends itself to Christian witness; but there are other reasons for it. We want to be open and candid with others, but we cannot often risk the interpersonal injury that may result from candor. We want to be "ourselves," but even if we know ourselves fully we cannot be the "real me" constantly, totally. So the demand for an authentic lifestyle has to be compromised by the genuine need for individual privacy and by society's need for civility and order.

The English and American Puritans were rather severe and solemn Christians to whom theatre was immoral—precisely because theatre involved *pretense*, role-playing. Role-playing was considered deceitful, so acting was sinful. But the Puritans wore masks too. The smug ones wore a godly costume that masked deep insecurities and the sin of self-righteousness.

If in real life we take on roles, trying on one mask after another—can theatre be so wrong? The stage gives people the opportunity to try on their masks in a safe setting. They can try on behaviors they wouldn't attempt in real life. That may be cathartic, or even exhilarating; and this is not immoral if the play as a whole has a positive effect on its audience. As a result of this showcased role-playing, the players gain a new understanding of human behavior, or a new self-awareness.

So it isn't surprising that theatre has the power to involve and absorb us, to suck us into the action, even sometimes to blur the distinction between the stage and life.

Understanding Art

But theatre is only one of the arts. We need to define art, ask whether art is godlike or God-ordained, and consider some of the ways theatre differs from arts like music, dance, painting, sculpture, and architecture.

Defining art is difficult. Clearly, art is a kind of self-expression, but a self-expression different from a curse, for example, or the invention of a plow. Some suggest the difference is that art is non-instrumental, non-functional, but this is overdrawn. Some functional things are at the same time aesthetically pleasing, such as a Frank Lloyd Wright building: Human expression may be functional and beautiful at the same time. And the first art was quite functional: dances designed to bring rain and painted pottery used to carry water. To be sure, art is not necessarily functional; it has value apart from whether you can wear it, use it to harvest beans, or eat from it. Indeed, some pottery is so marvelous you would not think of using it for a meal! We may say that as a culture accumulates art it is gathering artifacts that are not *solely* functional.

I like Suzanne Langer's definition of art because of its profound simplicity. Langer sees art, essentially, as feeling poured into form: "A work of art is an expressive form created for our perception through sense or imagination, and what it expresses is human feeling."[3] So a poem, a painting, or a concerto is a form within which an artist shares a perception of the world, or at least his or her small piece of the world, or an interpretation of that small piece of existence. Examine with me some important principles underlying a Christian understanding of art. (And I didn't say, an understanding of *Christian* art.)

First, art has value in itself but it cannot be given *ultimate* value. This contention is double-barreled. One implication is that an artifact need not be functional to be valuable. In Exodus 25, God is directing work on the tabernacle. He is just as painstakingly specific about the visual imagery, such as the crafting of the golden cherubim and candlesticks, as he is about the more functional elements of the tabernacle. Later, God gives detailed instructions for those who will embellish the priestly garments (Exodus 28). Clearly, God approves of human art, and beauty seems to be as important to him as practicality.

The other side of the coin is that we must never attach ultimate value to an artwork. The Christian knows that God alone is to be worshiped, not art. Those who speak of "art for art's sake" sometimes step over the line to blasphemy: They may worship the artifact rather than the One who inspired it. Which leads to our next contention, that *art must communicate.* An artwork must address someone besides its author meaningfully: Form must *inform.*

This means that art must be more than self-expression, a view that has taken us to extremes in modern times. Some artists have simply thrown paint at canvas or piled up junk in a mound and told us this was art; but not all self-expression is art. Stories abound of monkeys being set in front of a canvas and given paintbrushes, and encouraged to express themselves. The product of this monkey business was, we're told, considered art by some naive afficionados or critics.

A rather unique class of dramatists emerged since World War II, often grouped under the title "Theatre of the Absurd." Samuel Becket, Eugene Ionesco, and other writers of this stripe believe that human existence is meaningless, that life is a treadmill going · nowhere, and that we are deluded in thinking that we can communicate meaningfully. Eugene Ionesco, fantacizing one day about an English primer—he was learning the language—wrote a one-act, *The Bald Soprano*, in which the characters incessantly converse in banal nonsequiturs. But the paradox is that Ionesco is using words and lines to tell us that words are useless; if communication is impossible, why does he attempt it? To the extent that such a play does reach an audience, to that extent the playwright's thesis fails—because apparently some viewers are getting a message from the play. It is speaking to someone!

Thirdly, art forms are in themselves *morally neutral*. Beethoven's *Ode to Joy* or Paul Simon's music for *The Sounds of Silence* or a Rembrandt painting or a Da Vinci sculpture are vehicles for the expression of the artist's response to the world. We can judge the work's artistic worth by means of its form but we cannot judge its *moral* worth by its form; only by its *content*. And so we must disagree with those preachers who condemn all rock music as the work of the devil. They are confusing form and content. The music is form, the lyrics content; and any moral judgment has to be directed at the words, not the music. The message in the lyrics will vary from one piece of rock to another. Any contemporary art form, whether rock music, television drama, or motion pictures, may be used to elevate life or to denigrate it, as we see in the spate of plays and films exploiting racism and greed, sadism and violence. But also we've seen *Chariots of Fire, Gandhi,* and *Places in the Heart*.

So an artwork may be judged along two dimensions, form and message, or content. We determine the virtue of its form on the basis of artistic or technical standards; we judge its message or content on the basis of ethical or moral criteria which, for Christians, would be drawn from the Bible. However, there are some artworks, notably instrumental music (symphonies, concertos) where form and content are inseparable.

Some have attempted to join these two dimensions in a single set of criteria. Tolstoy, the great Christian novelist of Russia, suggested that these standards be used in judging an artwork: (1) Does it reveal a new side of life? (2) Is the form good and beautiful and consistent with its contents? And (3) Is the artist sincere?[4] And Francis Shaeffer, in a short essay, *Art and the Bible*, applies standards remarkably close to Tolstoy's: (1) technical excellence, (2) validity—close to Tolstoy's sincerity, (3) intellectual content, that is, the artist's world-view (or message), and (4) the integration of content and vehicle—Tolstoy's consistency. Shaeffer argues that the arts are not peripheral, but central to life. A Christian ought to use the arts to God's glory: ". . . not just as tracts, mind you, but as things of beauty for the praise of God. An art work can be a doxology in itself."[5]

The Mind of the Maker

The Bible is clear that God approves of art. But there is something else that makes art special, or makes the artist special: the principle of *imago dei*, the image of God (Genesis 1:27). At the creation of the world God blew the breath of life into Adam; more importantly, he created Adam *in his own image*.

What does that mean? What godlike qualities do we image? Dorothy Sayers, who has not only written some marvelous stories and plays but has written eloquently about the act of writing, answers the question in *The Mind of the Maker*. She says that the author of Genesis sees in humans something "essentially divine, but when we turn back to see what he says about the original upon which the 'image' of God was modeled, we find only the single assertion, 'God created.' The characteristic common to God and man is apparently that: the desire and the ability to make things."[6] Elsewhere Sayers says that "man is never truly himself except when he is actively creating something,"[7] and Clyde Kilby suggests that "artistic creativity is perhaps the highest attainment of man."[8]

We have to use metaphors to try to describe God. Sayers contends that the metaphor, God-as-Father, is a very rich concept but is overused. God-as-Creator, less used, is possibly more enlightening as a description of how God is like us and how he works through us. The first thing we find God doing is creating: He is the Maker of Genesis 1. We too are makers, and as God created *ex nihilo* there is a sense in which we can also create

33

something *out of nothing*; not in a pure sense, to be sure, but by rearranging elements of matter we can produce new forms and images, new entities that were absent before. "A million buttons," Sayers writes, "stamped out by a machine, even though they may be exactly alike, are not the same button; with each separate act of making, an entity has appeared in the world that was not there before."[9]

If this is true of buttons, how much more true with an *Antigone* or a *Death of a Salesman*? Each performance is unique in itself, different from every other performance of that play; but even if that were not so, the use of ten million words, all previously known to us, in the clever arrangement of dialogue, directions, and scenes to produce an *Antigone* or a *Death of a Salesman*, would seem to be an *ex nihilo* creation. Sayers: "It is the artist who, more than other men, is able to create something out of nothing. A whole artistic work is immeasurably more than the sum of its parts."[10] But this kind of invention is not merely a rearrangement of matter: "The amount of matter in the universe is limited, and its possible rearrangements, though the sum of them would amount to astronomical figures, is also limited. But no such limitation of numbers applies to the creation of works of art."

So true. Have you ever listened to a delightful new tune, asking yourself, "Isn't there some limitation to the invention of songs? There are just so many notes in the scale—why is it that the possible ways of arranging those notes are never exhausted?" We never seem to "use up" the possiblities for arranging notes in music, arranging words in poetry, stories, or plays, or arranging line and colors in painting and sculpture.

Jacob Bronowski argues that there's a single creative process, alike in the arts and sciences, which is "the discovery of a hidden likeness," another way of describing metaphor, and the scientist or artist

> creates a unity by showing the likeness.
>   The act of creation is therefore original; but it does not stop with its originator. The work of art or science is universal because each of us re-creates it. We are moved by the poem, we follow the theorem because in them we discover again and seize the likeness which their creator first seized. The act of appreciation reenacts the act of creation; and we are (each of us) actors, we are interpreters of it.[11]

All of which suggests an exalted view of human imagination, for the human artist is doing what the divine artist does best in the creative process. We are called to create as artists and to re-create as spectators. As my friend and colleague Betsy Morgan writes,

> . . . when an artist or craftsperson is attending to his/her task, the maker is participating in what it means to be created in God's image. The Jews who perceived, embellished and arranged the story of Joseph, Christ who confronted the Pharisees with stories, the sculptor who captures the graceful roundness in a marble orb, and the furniture maker who rubs the table top with oil so that the chaotic squiggles of spalted maple forever attest to the mystery of trees—all of these persons body forth in dynamic metaphor that expresses, but can never contain or replace it, the mystery of what drove God to make it all happen.[12]

Which brings us to the second theological dynamic informing and explaining the arts, and theatre. We have discussed creation; now *incarnation*.

Incarnation and Theatre

The Incarnation of God-in-Christ is exciting. We're told that "the Word became flesh and dwelt among us" (John 1:14) and that "in Christ God was reconciling the world to himself" (2 Corinthians 5:19). And Paul tells us that Christ Jesus,

> though he was in the form of God, did not count equality with God a thing to be grasped, but emptied himself, taking the form of a servant, being born in the likeness of men. And being found in human form he humbled himself and became obedient unto death, even death on a cross (Philippians 2:6-8).

Incarnation (Latin, *in carnus*) simply means "in the flesh." This role play, Jesus "taking the form of a servant," was an incarnation of God's love, embodied on earth. How marvelously concrete, this God-in-Christ, yet how mysterious! The British producer-director, E. Martin Browne, has written,

> The most important thing of all about drama for us Christians is that it partakes of the nature of incarnation . . . that the

coming of God to earth as man, the Word made flesh, is the climax of all human development in all fields. . . . So we see the Incarnation as God's use of the dramatic form in human history, as God's action in human life."[13]

Actually the Bible records two incarnations. The first was the creation of the world, when God blew the breath of life into his organic creations and pronounced it all "good." We are told specifically that God made man and woman "in his own image" (*imago dei*). Clearly, this doesn't mean physical image: At the moment the most obvious attribute of God was his talent as creator, as Maker. So we have to respect and revere that talent for making, that gift for imaging and imagining, indeed, for doing art, that God has given us.

The second Incarnation, centuries later, took place at Bethlehem. One might even say that this second Incarnation was necessary because the first one didn't "take," as a vaccination doesn't take, meaning that despite the divine reflection in human beings, they sinned; and after the Fall came the Advent. But it was not the Maker-ability that didn't take. Genesis 6:5 tells us that the imagination of men's minds was devoted to evil; that is, human beings had plenty of creative talent but they were using it for the wrong purposes. And so followed Sodom and Gommorah, the deluge, the warnings of the prophets, and when all that failed, the coming of a Redeemer. In Christ we see the extent to which God was willing to intervene historically. In Greek the word for drama (*dran*) means something done, a deed. Bethlehem and what followed was an ongoing drama, theological theatre at its best.

As a result of God's action in and through Jesus Christ, we have not only a part of God in us, or a number of attributes— whatever is implied by *imago dei*—but something of God's Son as well. (Matthew 25:40; Ephesians 3:17; Philippians 1:20-21) The pattern repeats itself in art: we are co-creators as we mold clay, paint a landscape, draw a cartoon, write a poem, or act in a play. We put something of ourselves into our works. If God through Christ indwells us then something of God shines through, visible to others, often despite ourselves, as a lamp beams through the slats in a wicker basket. (Which is an important biblical image for artists—see Matthew 5:15.)

Figure 1 illustrates the incarnational process, in terms of God-in-Christ working in us and through our relationships and art works.

36

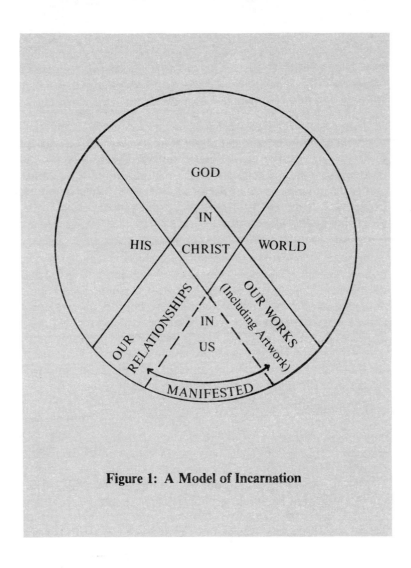

Figure 1: A Model of Incarnation

Each art is incarnational. The mind of the maker embodies an idea, using some kind of vehicle, form, or medium. Theatre and dance seem to express incarnation more acutely than other art forms since they are enacted in and through a physicality—live bodies—at the moment when the work is shown to an audience. In contrast, a drawing or painting is created previous to the spectator's glance; similarly, a novel or poem is written in time past.

But theatre is a *present* action. To fully apprehend a play's message it will not do to read a playscript or listen later to an audiotape of the performance. It may be more stimulating to watch a videotape, but even then you will lose something. It is much better to be where the people with real bodies are performing.

Theatre works largely because of its specificity, its concreteness. It may show a fragment of life in all its detail. Even without scenery there are the actors' faces, smudged with makeup and lined with emotion; the nuances of vocal inflection; the gestures and little movements that speak eloquently of determination, hesitation, or apprehension; the pauses that speak volumes; the absorbing details of story and character that engross us.

Theatre builds on the natural tendency for ideas to seek embodiment. Spiritual beings want to be enfleshed, and ideas are, in a broad sense, spiritual. Consider the feeling an author has when an idea in his or her mind thrashes about, demanding release. C. S. Lewis writes of when "there bubbles up every now and then the material for a story" that the inspired writer simply has to pour into a form, whether it be verse or prose, poem or play. "It is now a thing inside him pawing to get out. He longs to see that bubbling stuff pouring into that Form as the housewife longs to see the new jam pouring into the clean jam jar."[14]

From the other end, where the audience sits, there is also the need for embodiment. We want our abstractions fleshed out, concepts explained by means of clever anecdotes, parables, and analogies. How many of us have sat in classrooms—or even in church—thirsting for just one concrete example in a desert of high-level abstractions and not-so-glittering generalities? They said of Jesus that he taught nothing without a parable (Matthew 13:34), a model for effective communicating that many people today need to follow. Using the parable as an art form, Jesus raised it to a higher power of meaning.

Incarnation works from both ends in the theatrical event. From the creator's end there is the chain of feelings, or an Idea expressed in dramatic form, that proceeds from the creator-playwright through director and designer in and through the actors to the audience. (The birthing of an Idea, which requires a gestation period, takes place on stage—right out in public!)

From the viewer's end, incarnation works by creating the means by which an audience can identify with the living Idea through the playwright's characters. More on this later.

Religious Vs. Christian Theatre

The idea of incarnation suggests some components for a serious Christian theatre. In his essay, "Mimesis and Incarnation," Thomas Howard suggests that an incarnational view entails these notions: "It would affirm the immediate (because it believes in the Incarnation); it would affirm the transcendent (because it believes in the Logos); it would see the commonplace as the vehicle of ultimacy . . . and it would insist on the public character of significance. . . ."[15]

Good theatre does all of the above. *Oedipus* or *Hamlet* or Thornton Wilder's *Our Town* affirm the transcendent (that which is spiritual or eternal) within the immediacy of the setting, characters, and story; and they deal with the commonplace, particularly *Our Town*, which describes the ordinary lives of a few New England villagers—but how marvelously! And these plays make certain themes relatively public (clear, that is), as Howard says, unlike the glossolalia Paul warns us about in 1 Corinthians 14. Howard's criteria would exclude plays which are too esoteric to be lucid, too ethereal to be relevant, too exotic or bizarre to connect with human experience, or those with an individual vision too narrow to be understood.

But the idea of incarnation imposes additional standards. First, we have to look for an honest, authentic self-expression in the Christian artist. Tolstoy's term for it is sincerity; Francis Shaeffer's is validity; mine is *integrity*. We would expect a Christian to write from experience, of course, and to write nothing but the bold truth; thus, to be prophetic and passionate, not silly, sentimental, or superficial. It almost goes without saying that a Christian playwright is motivated by something other than fame and fortune.

Another component of a distinctive Christian art form is the *redemptive* element. This leads me to attempt to make the distinction between *religious* and *Christian* theatre.

Most serious theatre, if not all, has been religious. Its parameters are outlined in the questions that Ernest Ferlita uses to characterize *The Theatre of Pilgrimage*: Where did I come from? What am I? Where am I going?[16] Ferlita—for the purpose of his study—excludes some plays that fail to consider all three questions, but I would assume a play to be *religious* if it seriously considers at least one. Further, let's say that any drama is religious *that helps us examine our identity as created beings on earth*. Playwrights from Aeschylus and Sophocles to Ibsen and Shaw, Williams and Wilder, have displayed characters wrestling with the identity-question, "What am I meant to be and to do?": Oedipus and King Lear, Hamlet and Joan of Arc, Hedda Gabler, Willy Loman, Blanche Dubois, and George Antrobus.

So often on the modern stage the answers given to the identity-question are murky and confused: The audience is left totally befuddled and distraught. Many authors write characters who set out on a holy quest for the meaning of life; but the characters wander unfulfilled and frustrated, and their disillusion and despair affects the audience. At curtain's end, the characters remain mired in sin and guilt, or simply hopelessness.

There is much in the modern theatre that enlightens; very little that actually *ennobles*. Still, it's worth buying a ticket to modern classics like *Streetcar, Zoo Story*, or *Waiting for Godot*. These are honest attempts to grapple with identity in a difficult world; they are statements of meaning, or about the absence of it, and they are *religious* theatre; but not necessarily *Christian*.

If an artist has no answers to the question of identity, not even a partial one, then he or she is not functioning as a Christian artist. It is not enough to be honest; one must write from a Christian worldview to be a Christian artist. Nancy Tischler says that the Christian artist

> . . . could end his plays, not in futility and despair, but with a recognition that there is a power that can save and heal man and guide him so that he need not live in chaos . . . the Christian artist could emphasize salvation as well as sin, peace as well as turmoil, certainty as well as doubt.[17]

The key is the redemptive element. The incarnational element evokes the redemptive, as God's work in the world was and is redemption. Whether or not a play contains anything explicitly religious, any biblical characters, priests or ministers, any "God-talk" or any conversions, the play should warm us or heal us somehow, ennoble or enable us, or raise us to a higher power of understanding and faith.

But we need to avoid that drama that cheats the audience out of its own creative work. Art and incarnation are similar in their obliqueness; as Emily Dickinson puts it, "They tell all the truth but tell it slant." And Jerry Gill: "The incarnation, like a work of art, creates a 'space' within which the creator expresses the divine

40

character and intention in embodied form, inviting and encouraging an authentic and responsible commitment on the part of the persons being addressed."[18] We mustn't deny the audience the chance to draw its own conclusions. Good drama is like the operating room in MASH. "Close for us," we say to the audience, and take our bows.

Does the Christian playwright "preach"? Yes, in the sense of sharing values—none of us can avoid that, and Stanislavsky once described the stage as a pulpit—but not in the sense of explicit moralizing (which, more than anything, turns off a modern audience). The message should come through the logical development of action and authentic characters; as in real life, not through *lines said* as much as through *lives lived*.

Divine Comedy?

In popular thinking, tragic plays end sadly; comedies end happily. The classical definitions were more profound, however. Greek tragedies were plays depicting public events involving nobility, and written in verse; there was a protagonist-hero caught in the grip of fate and/or trapped by his own tragic "flaw". Comedies were plays depicting private or domestic events, ordinary people rather than nobility, and generally written in prose. Tragic plays often end badly, describing, in Chaucer's language,

> . . . hym that stood in great prosperitee,
> And is yfallen out of heigh degree
> Into myserie, and endeth wrechedly.

Comedies tended, and tend, to end happily; indeed, there is often a marriage—or even two or three—at the end of a comedy. And if there isn't a marriage between a young couple, there is at least some kind of resolution, some happy compromise, or the solution to a difficult problem.

Tragedy and comedy can be distinguished in relation to the cycle of nature and the element of hope. The sequence of the four seasons consists of birth or rebirth (spring), growth and struggle (summer and fall), death (winter), and again, rebirth. Classical tragedy takes us through struggle to a wintry death, whereas comedy completes the cycle through rebirth, or resurrection. Figure 2 shows the relationship of tragedy and comedy to the natural cycle.

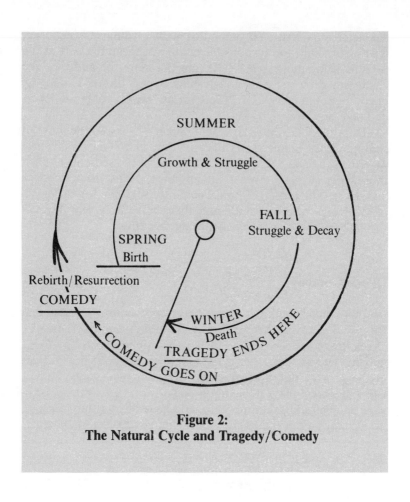

Figure 2:
The Natural Cycle and Tragedy/Comedy

Unlike tragedy, comedy may end sadly, but not badly. Among Shakespeare's plays, *King Lear* is the one "tragic" play that may be a divine comedy. *Macbeth, Othello, Hamlet* and the others end badly. We find in Iago and Macbeth no repentance and no redeeming grace. We come away with a sense of waste. But King Lear suffers and then repents of the way he's treated his daughter, Cordelia, and through her loving care he has a spiritual rebirth. Although he is about to die, Lear is humble and appreciative, with a very different attitude than he originally had. *King Lear* ends sadly, but not badly. We are left with an exalted feeling, what I would call *hope*. Comedy has hope and tragedy lacks hope; at any rate, I would not call a really hopeful play tragic.

This is not to say that the comic hero avoids suffering. As Nelvin Voss has demonstrated so well,[19] the comic faith-hero is, like Christ, both victim and victor, suffering servant and triumphant hero. But when it is dark enough you can see the stars; or, in the words of the black preacher, "It's Friday . . . but Sunday's comin'!" That's hope. If Christ is our model we have to go on from the trial before Pilate, and even beyond Golgotha to the resurrection. "Christianity," theatre scholar George Steiner writes, "is an anti-tragic vision of the world." And he adds that Christianity

> . . . leads the soul toward justice and resurrection. The Passion of Christ is an event of unutterable grief, but it is also a cipher through which is revealed the love of God for man. . . . Being a threshold to the eternal, the death of a Christian hero can be an occasion of sorrow, but not for tragedy."[20]

And so the fine verse dramatist, Christopher Fry, has written that comedy is "an escape, not from truth but from despair: a narrow escape into faith."[21]

When we think of drama celebrating the martyrdom of a Joan of Arc, a Bonhoeffer, or a Martin Luther King, Jr., we see the wisdom in the above testimony. At the end of the play there is grief, but also great hope and joy! For the gospel is undefeated, truth is undaunted by death. So a play like *St. Joan* or *A Man for All Seasons* is a divine comedy, Christian theatre at its best. For comedy is not defined as whatever makes us laugh, but what surmounts both tears and laughter to reveal and to heal.

How Theatre Works

Theatre's diversity is amazing. We go from "simple" one-person shows—Hal Holbrook as *Mark Twain*, Tom Key as *C. S. Lewis*—to enormously complex literary and dramatic masterpieces like George Bernard Shaw's *Man and Superman* involving a full evening in the theatre, or the Oberammergau Passion Play, involving a full day of performance. Or, contrast the elaborately rehearsed production of an *Our Town* or *King Lear* with the frenetic spontaneity of a "happening" or "die-in" to promote some cause, or the improvisations of a clever troupe doing drama informally on the street. They are all theatre, but what holds them together? What makes them all "work"?

The root of the word *theatre* in Greek is "seeing-place" or "viewing-place"; and it may be related to the Greek, *thauma*, a wonder. The theatre was a wonderful place for seeing a physical drama, but also for gaining inward vision or *insight*. And the Greek word for drama, *dran*, means to do: Drama is something done, a deed. So one of the keys to drama is action. Even as we are known more by our deeds than by words (James), so theatre exists as a place where deeds may be viewed and not simply words heard.

Of course, your first task as dramatist is to interest an audience: to entertain. I refer to entertainment in a broad sense. We say of a performance, "It was so entertaining!" and we tell our friend that we saw a comedy that made us laugh. Serious plays are not very "entertaining" in that sense, but they do entertain in a broad sense: They keep the audience interested or intrigued enough to keep watching, they "work" in the way that theatre must work to exist at all.

We have said that art is a distilling of experience, a pouring of felt-life into form. A drama is a literary form; the play on its stage is the theatrical form. A well-staged play is very compelling; we're absorbed by it. How so? These terms—illusion, conflict, and identification—give us a sense of how and why theatre works.

First, *illusion*. Understand that art and life are never the same. Life and theatre are never identical, no matter how "realistic" the play is, no matter how naturalistic and detailed the stage is, no matter how many dustballs and doilies are on the furniture. At some level of consciousness we know it's a play we're watching. Although we may become so involved that we consciously forget that fact, we're jogged back to reality by the sneeze of a seatmate, a bit of lighting that doesn't work, a muffed line, or the fact that the curtain is drawn—and perhaps a bit late. But generally we're aware anyway.

But, you argue, actual life experience may indeed be staged! You tell me to tape-record a conversation at the intersection of Broad and Main Streets, and transcribe it so that we have a script. Also, you photograph the real people at Broad and Main so that we are able to costume our actors identically; and then if we build what appears to be that street corner on our stage we have a "slice of life."

Not so: Even then we know it's "only" a play. After all, we paid our money for tickets and we have read the program. Per-

44

haps we know the actors. And we have not, after all, culled a random conversation from the street—we have *selected* one. Selectivity is an artistic judgment.

Moreover, this conversation from Broad and Main will turn out to be a very dull play; even if it is close to "real life," it may not be art, after all. When you pretend that an ordinary conversation is art you disappoint people. They come to the theatre expecting more. The role of the artist is to enhance, elaborate, selectively enlarge ordinary behavior, ordinary experience. So theatre is not life, but a selective enlargement of life; and the result is something much broader and more profound than ordinary life. Gardner writes that "theatre arises from an audience's exposure to the extra-real." Theatre, someone said, is a lie more truthful than life itself.

This is done through illusion: The theatre is a house of magic. In effect we create an agreement between actors and audience, a compact. They agree mutually to suspend disbelief for the duration of the performance. The actor tells the viewer, "If you believe I am who I say I am, we'll be able to create a very special world." If the viewer agrees, theatre happens. If there is something that doesn't work in the script or in the performance, something "hokey," then it doesn't happen. The play isn't credible. Or if there is something in the viewer that prevents him from wholeheartedly entering into this invented world, it doesn't happen.

There are different kinds of theatre illusion. Some plays are very naturalistic, or *representational*. The actors don't seem to notice or need the audience: they pretend it doesn't exist. Other plays are *presentational*. The actors are not only aware of the audience but address it directly; or they engage in nonrealistic acts such as breaking into song or chanting in unison, things that don't normally happen in life-experience. When this is done deliberately to create an aesthetic distance, to keep the audience "critical" so they may learn their lessons from the play instead of identifying emotionally with it, the result is often defined as "Epic Theatre."

Today we tend to think of the more representational or "realistic" theatre as traditional, as the mainstream. Actually the reverse is true. Presentational theatre is the mainstream, running from the ancient Greeks to the present; representational theatre is more of a modern aberration. But the latter has become very popular since Ibsen, and a number of great modern playwrights,

45

such as Arthur Miller and Tennessee Williams, have worked with it. But in both cases theatre works by illusion; in the one case the illusion is frankly invented, in the other disguised. The one is overt: We are invited to imagine or even told what to imagine. The other is covert: We are ignored. We are left to assume that it's not a play, but life itself on stage.

Second, *conflict*. Conflict is engrossing. It interests us. We're a competitive race: Conflict excites us. The one play sometimes cited as an exception to the rule that every play has conflict is Thornton Wilder's *Our Town*. Perhaps this play proves Wilder's genius, for he was able to defy convention and create a moving drama without overt conflict. But, almost universally, drama involves conflict.

There are various types of dramatic conflict: conflict between individuals, between an individual and a group or a society, between groups, or between the individual and a set of circumstances (or caught between a rock and a hard place!) Conflict presumes obstacles, and these may be the character's own limitations (internal) or the opposition of someone, some group, or some external force. And so suspense: Will the hero or heroine manage to overcome these obstacles and realize some objective, gain some goal? In a broader, religious sense, will this person's mission in life be attained or thwarted? We want to know!

Sometimes we have two or more of these types of conflict in a particular play. Miller's *Death of a Salesman* is an example. Willy Loman's values come into conflict with those of other members of his family, especially his wife; also, he comes into conflict with circumstances, for he's getting older and losing his touch as a salesman, and the boss may want to replace him with a younger man. And within Willy there is a conflict between his dreams of success and material fulfillment on the one hand, and his own drab achievements, or lack of them, on the other. Often the internal conflicts are more engrossing than the external ones.

Thirdly, *identification* makes theatre work. We speak of vicarious experience: A reader/viewer may enter into the experience of a character in a novel, a movie, or a play. The character's experience substitutes for his or her own.

The bond between viewer and character may take two forms. One is the bond in which the viewer identifies with a character who is very much like himself or herself; so the identification happens *because of* that affinity. After all, we like to see ourselves, whether in a mirror or on a stage. A second sort of bond occurs when the viewer identifies with a character unlike himself or herself. We do this because we admire that person or *aspire to be like* that person. It may take the form of hero-worship: When I was a child I identified with Superman and even used him in my dreams to ward off monsters.

I may not like any of the characters in *Death of a Salesman*, but I may *be like* Willy Loman in some ways. Perhaps I have experienced family tensions similar to those in his family, or I too have been frustrated by the success fantasy. On the other hand, I am very unlike George Bernard Shaw's heroine, *Joan of Arc*. I have not heard "voices," I have not led troops into battle, and I haven't been accused of witchcraft or heresy. But I can identify with Joan because I admire her courage, her stubborn adherence to conviction, and her bravery under fire. Also, I envy her fierce faith. So my bond with Willy Loman is forged through *alikeness* but I am bonded to Joan through *aspiration*. Either way, the identification works largely at a subconscious level.

Conclusion

Illusion, conflict, and identification are keys to theatre's power to involve an audience. These functioned in the Passion Play my student reported, and with the woman in Central Park who when she heard stage thunder began to don her rain hat.

Theatre works through a "mutual suspension of disbelief," an illusion that seizes us and won't let us go until we rouse and shake ourselves and, reeling, stagger out the aisle and into the lobby, lounge, or narthex. Such is the power of good theatre to amuse and hold us, warm us and inspire us; indeed, to envelop us! Let us not settle for anything less because we are *only* doing religious theatre, or performing in a church.

Yes, theatre works. So work with it!

3

From Pageant Wagons to the Cotton Patch Gospel

Is there anyone who doesn't love a parade? Perhaps so—the Zacchaeus who's too short to see, or the claustrophic individual—but for most of us, parades are exciting. We enjoy the Pasadena rose parade on New Year's Day or the local Memorial Day shindig, with the convertibiled mayor and the Fire Department on hook-and-ladder proudly following the high school band down Main Street.

Watching the fourteenth century medieval pageant wagons was like watching a parade. Each of the craft guilds built their own wagon-stage, drawn by horses or oxen: It was a mobile stage indeed. The plays, called *mysteries* because they had to do with faith and faith was a mystery, each represented some Bible event. They were performed in sequence, according to Bible history, and thus were often called *cycle plays*. Often the cycle began with a play about the creation of the world and ended with the last judgment.

Each play had its wagon, and the wagons followed each other through town on a given feast day, usually the holy day called Corpus Christi, so that anyone standing at a given location could witness the entire sequence of performances—if he or she had the stamina required to stand for hours. Imagine the excitement of an illiterate populace, lacking TV, radio, newspapers, and modern forms of entertainment, when the spring festival finally arrived and the annual cycle was to be presented. On Corpus Christi day the festivities began before dawn, as the players hitched up their oxen, arranged their carts, and put their costumes in order. Historian E. Martin Browne describes the event as it may have happened at York, England:

> Outside the wall of the city we see a scene of great animation. Where the forecourt of the railroad station now stands there is a rough grassy sward. It is called "Pageant Green." On it hundreds of men are running hither and thither with great verve and purpose; and into it a series of great carts, all of them with different superstructure, some one story high, some two, all elaborately decorated, are being pulled from sheds that surround its edge.[1]

According to Browne, there were twelve stations or stopping-places around York, and the forty-eight plays comprising the York cycle were performed from 4:30 a.m. until dusk in the evening. What a spectacle!

But the medieval cycle plays didn't emerge full-blown from the head of a Christian muse, following centuries of no theatre during the Dark Ages. They evolved from two developments in Catholic Christendom during the ninth and tenth centuries: the dramatic possibilities in the Lenten season and the tropes that were being inserted into the services, the Hours and the Mass.

The church calendar provided an incentive to drama; the events of Passion Week in particular lent themselves to visual demonstration. Often the church arranged an elaborate procession on Palm Sunday, with a figure upon a donkey, riding from the city walls to the cathedral. On Good Friday the priests might take a cross, wrap it in cloth, and place it inside a symbolic tomb in the chancel, from which it was taken triumphantly on Easter morning. Drama had an affinity with other seasonal events and church symbols and traditions, but Lent was the most opportune time.

Also, there was a type of dialogue in the Mass: antiphonal songs, which were divided between individuals, or between a soloist and a choir. And then tropes, or insertions into an existing text, began to creep into the Mass. These

> ... first took the form of lengthened musical passages, originally of the final syllable of the "Allelulia." Eventually this extended melody became so elaborate that words were added, one sylla-

ble for each note, as an aid to memory . . . It is from an Easter trope that the birth of drama is usually traced.[2]

This was the famous *Quem Queritas*, found in the introductory portion of the Mass about 925. These are the lines, translated from the original Latin:

ANGEL: Whom seek ye in the tomb, O Christians?
THE THREE MARYS: Jesus of Nazareth, the crucified,
    O Heavenly Beings.
ANGEL: He is not here, he is risen as he foretold.
    Go and announce that he is risen from the tomb.

We are fortunate in having a complete text of the stage directions for this seminal drama, which are a part of the *Concordia Regularis*, prepared about 980 by St. Ethelwold, Bishop of Winchester, in order to regulate English church procedures:

While the third lesson is being chanted, let four brethren vest themselves. Let one of these, vested in an alb, enter as though to take part in the service, and let him approach the sepulchre without attracting attention and sit there quietly with a palm in his hand. While the third response is chanted, let the remaining three follow, and let them all, vested in copes, bearing in their hands thuribles with incense, and stepping delicately as those who seek something, approach the sepulchre. These things are done in imitation of the angel sitting in the monument, and the women with spices coming to annoint the body of Jesus. When therefore he who sits there beholds the three approach him like folk lost and seeking something, let him begin in a dulcet voice of medium pitch to sing *Quem Queritas*? And when he has sung it to the end, let the three reply in unison *Jesum Nazarenum*. So he, *Non est hic, surrexit sicut praedixerat. Ite, nuntiate quia surrexit a mortuis.* At the word of his bidding let those three turn to the choir and say *Alleluia! Resurrexit Dominus!* This said, let the one, still sitting there and as if recalling them, say the anthem *Venite et videte locum.* And saying this, let him rise and lift the veil, and show them the bare place of the cross, but only the cloth laid there in which the cross was wrapped.

The drama is concluded with another anthem, a hymn, *Te Deum Laudamus* (We praise thee, O God), and the ringing of the church bells.

With *Quem Queritas* we have impersonation, with some coaching provided for the priest-actors taking the roles of the angel and the three Marys; and we have minimal properties (palm, incense, spices, veil) and costuming (alb and copes). This was not dramatic "realism." As Wickham suggests,

> It was clearly intended that the congregation should be confronted with a double image. The Marys are men, not women. They wear copes, not fashionable female attire or historical "period" dress. The dialogue is in Latin, not English; chanted, not spoken; and punctuated with hymns and anthems.[3]

But the climax is the *Te Deum*, a magnificent praise-hymn in which actors and audience joined; and what seems artificial or contrived in terms of theatre becomes a joyous ritual celebration of a pivotal event in Christian history. "The result," Wickham writes, "is liturgical music-drama, for which the theatre is the basilica itself, the occasion a festival of rejoicing."

The development of the trope to full-fledged drama took place over decades. Soon *Quem Queritas* was expanded, dialogue added, the impersonation grown fuller and richer; then other events of the Passion were inserted; pretty soon tropes and related mini-dramas were inserted into the Advent services and other church occasions; and eventually these liturgical dramas spread throughout Europe. By the middle of the twelfth century a more spectacular liturgical drama evolved, spreading beyond the altar and chancel: "Mansions," or simple set-pieces like the throne of God or a shed and manger for the nativity were placed around the nave of the cathedral, where the standing congregation could follow the action from one location to another, as a whole series of plays was presented. Gradually the dialogue departed from the biblical narrative, additional action and business was surmised and inserted by creative people, and the language was "vulgarized"; no longer Latin, it became vernacular, with bits of humor and contemporary references added. Cohen describes the result:

> As time passed, its dazzling display of costumes, set pieces, and "acting" performances was less and less tied to the sacred office of the Mass which had given it birth, more and more aimed at entertainment. The next step was perhaps inevitable: the medieval liturgical theatre outgrew the Mass, outgrew the liturgy, outgrew the production capabilities of the clergy, outgrew the cathedral itself—and burst forth upon the medieval marketplace.[4]

The progression from church to village square was hastened by the edict issued by Pope Innocent III in A.D. 1210. Because of increasingly secular elements, these dramas were no longer "fit" for liturgical use: The Pope ordered the players out of his cathedrals! Outside, the plays retained their religious essence but more theatrical elements were added; and the cycles developed.

The cycle plays were the most popular form of entertainment during the Middle Ages in England, and a highly effective form of religious instruction. The town's craft guilds sponsored and prepared the plays. The city fathers or aldermen allocated plays to suitable guilds: The shipwrights, for example, or the water-drawers guild, would be assigned the play of Noah's ark; the play of the Magi, requiring crowns and golden jewelry, would be assigned to the goldsmiths, and the crucifixion to the carpenters or the nail-makers. The city corporation established the order of performance, the stations, and the rules under which the entire pageant would be given.

These Bible plays, or *mysteries*, were extremely popular during the heyday of Medieval theatre in the fourteenth, fifteenth, and sixteenth centuries. Other forms of staging were used besides wagons: Long outdoor stages were common in the continental towns of France, Spain, and Italy, as well as occasional performances in the round or in courtyards.

The subject matter for the mysteries were either Bible events or imagined events based on interpretations of the Bible, such as plays of the Last Judgment. The Creation, Adam and Eve, Cain and Abel, Abraham and Isaac, and Noah, were the favorite scenes from the Old Testament; in the New, the stories of the Nativity, Crucifixion, and Resurrection were most often dramatized. Old Testament stories were chosen both for their dramatic qualities and their ability to foreshadow the coming of Christ. These were didactic or teaching plays; they explained and interpreted the Bible and salvation-history to the populace.

But the mysteries were very entertaining. Spectacular effects were added: The more sophisticated platform stages permitted actors (angels, perhaps) to be "flown" to the stage, hell's mouth was represented with a fearsome maw, mad demons and pitchforks, and the smell of burning flesh, produced by igniting animal carcasses. One medieval notebook indicates that someone was paid for "setting the world on fire."

The humorous element can be illustrated with *The Second Shepherd's Play,* by an unknown Wakefield "master," and by *The*

Crucifixion, from the York cycle. In the former, three shepherds grumble about their hard lot, watching their flocks at night on the moor. As they fall asleep a prankster, Mak, steals one of their sheep, carries it to his hut, and with the help of his wife, hides it in a cradle. The shepherds search Mak's hut unsuccessfully; they are about to leave when one suggests that they offer gifts to the infant in Mak's cradle! When the baby is discovered to be their lost sheep, the shepherds toss Mak in a blanket for punishment. An angel appears to them to announce the birth of Christ, and they repair to the manger to honor him. So the farcical element is woven into the serious Advent theme of Christ's coming at Bethlehem.

The York *Crucifixion* "brings the obscene and blasphemous face to face with divinity," as Sarah Payne suggests.[5] Four Roman soldiers prepare the cross on which Christ is to be executed, apparently oblivious to their victim: They go about their work as if he is not present. Instead, they complain about their task:

> SECOND SOLDIER: And certainly I am near exhausted
>   So long have I borne under
> THIRD SOLDIER: This cross and I in two must part
>   Else breaks my back asunder.

As they work, they make callous comments like . . .

> FIRST SOLDIER: These saws shall rue him sore
>   For all his sauntering, soon.
> SECOND SOLDIER: Bad luck to them that him do spare
>   Till he to death be done.
> FIRST SOLDIER: Now raise him nimbly by the measure
>   And set him by the mortice here
>   And let him fall in all at once
>   So his bones break all asunder everywhere.

The play has a lot of grim humor, Payne suggests, and shows the striking contrast in attitudes of those involved in the execution:

> FIRST SOLDIER: Why carp ye so? Fasten on a cord
>   And tug him to by top and tail
> SECOND SOLDIER: Yes, *thou* commandest readily as a lord;
>   You can help to tail him, with ill hail
> FIRST SOLDIER: Now of course that shall I do
>   Full quickly as a snail.

53

Irreverent indeed: Yet the coarse joking strikes me as the kind of thing that insensitive soldiers—who had been through countless bloody crucifixions, "all in a day's work"—might have said. Payne contends that "the York play manages to lift the Crucifixion from sentimental piety to a stark human tragedy with comic overtones," and she quotes W. Moelwyn Merchant:

> For this mixture of the noble and the ridiculous, the comic, the sublime and tragic, is characteristic of the very nature of man . . . and both tragedy and levity are part of the same vision, of the bizarre dance macabre in which lady and jester, king and lean beggar dance together to the same end.[6]

The mysteries were the first of three major types of religious theatre in the Middle Ages. The others were the *miracle plays*, whose subjects were the saints or church heroes and heroines; and the *morality plays*, which taught appropriate behavior for Christian people and the way of salvation. We'll examine each type and apply the types to the body of plays we have available today as Christian dramatists. I find the medieval types useful as broad categories in which to classify modern drama.

Mysteries: Plays of Bible Events and Characters

We have already discussed some modern biblical plays in Chapters One and Two. Clearly, biblical drama is still popular with church audiences and is still being written. A list of the most popular writers of biblical drama would have to include, in this country, Amy Goodhue Loomis, Dorothy Clarke Wilson, Earl Reimer, and Don Mueller. British dramatists, notably Christopher Fry, R. H. Ward, and P. W. Turner, have developed profound biblical verse plays. Perhaps Don Mueller's *Eyes Upon the Cross*, a sequence of eight short Lenten plays, corresponds best to the medieval cycle plays.

From medieval times to now, there have been certain favorite biblical subjects. Aside from Advent and Lenten themes, about which hundreds of plays have been written, the notable favorites seem to be Jonah, Noah, and Job. Numerous scripts on these stories exist, with a few representing attempts to make the theme commercially successful. Examples on the Noah theme: Obey's *Noah*, Odets' *The Flowering Peach*, and the musical *Two by*

Two, starring Danny Kaye in a brief New York run. Job has been given full-length treatment by Neil Simon in a modern analogue, *God's Favorite*, and more profoundly by Archibald MacLeish in *J.B.* And various Christian dramatists, including myself,[7] have written one-acts on Jonah, Job, and Noah.

It appears there is no end to the myriad possible dramatic interpretations. Jonah plays range from the comic Jewish idiom of Wolk Mankowitz' *It Should Happen to a Dog!* to the formalized chancel style of Olov Hartman in *Prophet and Carpenter*. George Ralph found some twenty-nine Jonah plays in the process of writing a dissertation.[8] He invented a classification system for the Jonah plays: six categories, ranging from comic treatments to didactic to liturgical to narrative-interpretative. The biblical treatments vary considerable in how far the writer departs from the biblical text and chronology. Jonah seems to be an endearing figure—due to his essential humanity, I suppose—and very attractive to dramatists.

Miracles, or Hero Plays

Scholars have referred to those plays having Christian saints as their subjects as *miracle plays*, for the saints were canonized as a result of having allegedly performed miracles. Few of the English miracles have survived, probably because of the Reformation and Protestant hostility to the Catholic saints. Miracle plays were numerous on the continent, however, and several have survived.

One of the earliest miracles, written in Latin and French by an Englishman, Hilarius, about A.D. 1100, is *The Miracle of Saint Nicholas*. In the play, a barbarian king gathers his property and commends it to the care of the image of St. Nicholas. Robbers, finding the door open, steal the king's treasure. The king returns, discovers that his gold is gone, and grieves before the image. St. Nicholas then goes to the robbers, and threatens to expose them. The robbers return the treasure and when the king finds it he rejoices and thanks the icon. St. Nicholas appears to him then and tells the king to praise God instead of the image. The king is converted.

Let us stretch our definition to say that miracle plays have as their subject, Christian heroes; so we'll include various historical plays and modern dramas about heroes of the faith. For example, several fine dramas about the legendary Joan of Arc, have been written—by Maxwell Anderson, George Bernard Shaw, and Jean Anhouilh, among others. Thomas Becket, the martyred Archbishop of Canterbury, has also become a popular subject, as plays by Anhouilh and T. S. Eliot attest. Over the past thirty years we have hero plays such as Bolt's *A Man for All Seasons* (Sir Thomas More), Osborne's *Luther* (treated somewhat unsympathetically), Berryhill's *The Cup of Trembling* and Anderson's *The Beams Are Creaking* (Dietrich Bonhoeffer), and my own *God Is My Fuehrer* (Martin Niemoeller). Norman Bert has written a fine play on the eighteenth century Quaker who contested slavery, *Woolman*. Albert Johnson, writing for drama trios at Redlands University, celebrated Roger Williams in *Roger Williams and Mary* and the pioneer missionary to Burma, Adoniram Judson, in *Conquest in Burma.*

The list goes on. Historical plays typically have large casts but some playwrights, like Albert Johnson, have chosen to use actors sparingly, devising ways of telling the story by having them "double" in various roles. Reducing the number to one, stirring monodramas, or "one-man shows" as they are often called, have been presented recently: Hal Holbrook doing Mark Twain and Lincoln, James Whitmore doing Harry Truman; and in terms of Christian heroes, C. S. Lewis and Father Damien have been subjects for monodramas. For shorter material, consider Everett Robertson's collection of *Monologues for Church*[9] which includes first-person stories told by the Christian explorer, David Livingston, and by Lottie Moon, pioneer missionary to China.

Biographical drama can be exciting, for truth *is* often stranger, more absorbing than fiction. Nothing in Christian literature can surpass the power of a dedicated life lived courageously for Jesus Christ and his kingdom. Take a Christian who's had to make some hard choices and who has suffered as a result yet remained true to his or her vision . . . and you have the recipe for inspiring, uplifting Christian theatre.

Moralities, or Plays About Human Conduct

The third class of plays to emerge during the Middle Ages—later than the other two—were the *moralities*. Such plays have to do with morals, human conduct, and, in particular, the way of salvation. Often they depict the clash between the vices and virtues for someone's soul. They use abstract characters rather than three-dimensional, realistic ones: Sloth, Lechery, Pride, Hope, Good Deeds, Charity, Confession, are examples. These plays are definitely didactic: They were meant to teach the audience a lesson about life and faith. The most famous, *Everyman*, begins with a moralistic Prologue:

> "The story saith: Man, in the beginning, look well, and take good heed to the ending, be you never so gay!"

And at the play's end a learned "Doctor" concludes, lest the auditors miss the point:

> "This moral man may have in mind.
> Ye hearers, take it of worth, old and young,
> And forsake Pride, for he deceiveth you in the end;
> And remember Beauty, Five Wits, Strength, and Discretion,
> They all at last do Everyman forsake,
> Save his Good Deeds there doth he take.
> But beware and they be small,
> Before God he hath no help at all."

Everyman, which dates from about 1500, concerns someone who is summoned by Death to make a reckoning. Everyman wants a companion to speak for him at the judgment and tries in vain to persuade his Kinsman, Strength, Goods, and others to accompany him. The play is about the way of salvation, and how one prepares for death.

Everyman's theology is of course medieval and very Catholic. It reflects the world view of medieval times: Human beings are corrupt sinners in desperate need of God's grace. Their end is the flames of hell unless they repent, confess their sins, and are granted absolution by the church. To assist in the process, penitential acts included rigorous confessions, pilgrimages, indulgences, and the intercession of the saints. Essentially, salvation was mediated only through the church and prompted by penitential *works*.

Since World War II Albert Johnson and certain others have revised *Everyman* to give it a more Protestant tone, with more emphasis on grace and love and less on works. The confession scene, which included a scourging in some early versions, has now been modified or eliminated. Today *Everyman* is sometimes written in the vernacular or performed in modern dress to give it more relevance, but it has a timeless message that needs to be heard again and again. There were many other morality plays during the late Middle Ages and early Renaissance but *Everyman* alone retains its popularity.

Two modern dramas have a close resemblance to *Everyman*. Ken Taylor's *This Is the End* was written for outdoor performance on the porch at Coventry Cathedral, England. Again the characters are abstract types with symbolic names: John Adamson and his wife Eve are central, and there is Death. The setting is a television studio doing a show much like "This Is Your Life," except that the emcee is someone in a skull mask and the show's new title is "This Is Your Death!"

Adamson is just moving through the audience, on his way to an appointment, when he is stopped by Death, who informs him that he is about to suffer a fatal thrombosis in exactly twenty-four minutes! Adamson, an ambitious young businessman whose life lacks strong values or a real focus, is given this time to talk to his mother and other persons who have meant something to him. He wants to discover what they believe about life and faith and thereby make some sense of his own death; but they have little to give him. Then Death comes again to a now pale and desperate Adamson. In contrast to *Everyman*, Death ends the show *without* providing any moral for the audience. There is an unstated lesson, of course, and the message is powerful—the audience being left to draw its own conclusions. But the play lacks the redemptive element in *Everyman*. It is tragic, religious drama at its best, and well worth doing—but not truly *Christian* theatre.

Eve McFall's *The Case Against Eve* uses a courtroom to frame the action. It's a mythical, nonrealistic setting, in which a modern housewife puts herself on trial for the failure to find meaning in life. She happens to be frustrated with her world of vacuum cleaners, endowment policies, social events, and a church that keeps one busy with activities but lacks spiritual depth. Eve finds meaning at last, with the help of a fisherman—son of a carpenter-turned repairman, and returns to the symbolic Garden with her husband, Adam. Appropriate scripture is inserted into the action, which consists of engaging vignettes linked by choric passages. The play is highly symbolic, well written, and concludes with a ringing affirmation of God's power to redeem and ennoble life . . . an excellent modern "Everywoman."

We have used plays as examples which are much like the Medieval moralities in their symbolism and abstract character-types. At another level of definition it is possible to speak of moralities as plays that simply deal with human conduct; that is, ethics, questions about right and wrong behavior. Broadly speaking then, hundreds of modern dramas are moralities. Characters making difficult moral choices—Joe Keller making the wrong choice in Miller's *All My Sons* or Walter Lee Younger finally making the right choice in Hansberry's *A Raisin in the Sun* are two examples. One is a tragedy of wasted life as Keller commits suicide, unable to live with his past; the other a comedy of hope and renewal for the black family leaving its Chicago ghetto.

Of course, some plays *defy classification*. A play may have a biblical setting but otherwise, in its mood and tone, seem like a morality; or a hero play may also demonstrate a moral lesson. Distinctions are arbitrary and break down easily: Often the best plays are too vibrant, too dynamic to be easily boxed and labeled.

Now I will define another term—but it's not a fourth type of drama; instead, a concept that cuts across all three categories.

Christ-Figures and Passion Plays

In Shakespearean London there were laws restricting play-wrights in terms of the language they could use. It could not be seditious in tone, and it could not invoke the deity. Consequently, playwrights skirted around the use of God's name. Shakespeare used substitute phrases. "There's a *divinity* that shapes our ends," Hamlet says. And Kent, in *King Lear*: "It is the *stars*, the stars above us, govern our condition." Juliet: ". . . that *heaven* should practise strategems upon so soft a subject as myself!"

In addition to restrictions on language, at various times and places playwrights have been prevented from putting divine personages on stage. The medieval dramatists represented God and Jesus in their plays, but later such representations were banned. Even as late as the early 1940s Dorothy Sayers, rehearsing her pioneering radio drama, *The Man Born to Be King*, which included Jesus as a character, found it necessary to hold rehearsals in private, without a live audience.

In the first half of the century, Christian playwrights often put Christ into plays in disguise, so that people could respond to him in a way that might evoke the lesson of Matthew 25:40, ". . . As you did it to one of the least of these my brethren, you did it to me." There is a Christ-figure, for example in Jewell Tull's popular play, *The Forgotten Man*, where Jesus appears to several

59

members of a church congregation as a mysterious stranger, a wanderer who, for a brief moment, manages to redeem and heal— and then leaves them, leaving his love behind. And there have been several dramatizations of Tolstoy's equally sentimental, endearing *Where Love Is, There God Is Also*,[10] the story of a cobbler who is expecting a heavenly visitor one night. Jesus doesn't physically appear, but the cobbler discovers that in fact our Lord called on him in the person of individuals whom the cobbler befriended.

Gradually the public attitude toward the actual representation of God and Jesus has liberalized. Mark Connelly's *Green Pastures* in the thirties, with its warm-hearted, quite human God, broke ground. And now, with George Burns playing God in the movies and actors appearing as Jesus Christ in film and in such plays as *Jesus Christ Superstar* and *Godspell*, we have a different scene entirely.

A *Christ-figure* (as opposed to Christ as a character) is someone in literature who strongly reminds one of Jesus Christ. Often it is that person's gentleness and compassion, or healing qualities, that creates the Christ-image; or it may be someone who suffers for other people or for a principle, as Jesus suffered, and who may die as a result. Modern critics have searched the world's literature for Christ-figures, finding them in diverse stories from Dostoevsky's *The Idiot* to Hemingway's *The Old Man and the Sea*. Some even find them in comic strips: The *Peanuts* interpreter, Robert L. Short, identified Snoopy as the Christ-figure![11]

Clearly a character must be more than a "nice guy" to be a Christ-figure. Coxe and Chapman's *Billy Budd*, based on the story by Melville, is well-written, engaging, and insightful. The central figure is Billy Budd, a gentle, innocent young seaman who has been pressed for duty aboard the *HMS Indomitable* in 1798. Billy is kind and good-natured and has a positive influence on everyone except for the Master-at-Arms, John Claggart, who constantly ridicules and provokes him. The turning point comes when Billy, who has a speech impediment, inadvertently strikes Claggart, who falls and suffers a fatal blow on the head. After painful deliberation by the ship's officers, many of whom want to acquit Billy, he is condemned to death by the law of the sea. As the play ends, Billy, about to swing at the yardarm, quells incipient mutiny among his shocked shipmates and echoes Jesus' words from the cross with his last cry: "God bless Captain Vere!" Powerful! Unhappily, it requires a large, all-male cast.

Rolf Hochhuth surprised the Western world with his carefully researched drama, *The Deputy*, in 1963. Heavily documented like a thesis, Hochhuth's play argues that the Pope and the Catholic hierarchy turned their collective back on the European Jews toward the end of World War II, despite having knowledge of the incredible holocaust. Riccardo Fontana is a Jesuit priest who struggles desperately to bring the plight of the Jews to the attention of the curia and the Pope. In a climactic scene Fontana, having failed to convince the Pope to issue a statement condemning Hitler's "final solution," pins the Jewish gold star to his own chest in the Pope's presence. Harshly, he remarks, "God shall not destroy his Church only because a Pope shrinks from his summons." The Pope stands stunned as Riccardo leaves his chamber.

Later Riccardo, pretending to be Jewish, has himself deported from Italy in a cattle car with Jews herded up by the SS. Arriving at Auschwitz, Riccardo spends several months trying to comfort the afflicted—he has been put to work at the crematorium by the infamous "Doctor" of Auschwitz. Ultimately, implicated in an abortive attempt by some friends conspiring to make an attempt on the Doctor's life, Riccardo is shot and killed.

The Deputy is a profound, controversial play. Certainly Riccardo takes on the suffering servant role of Christ, and although the drama is intended to indict the Catholic hierarchy, it succeeds in touching the audience by means of Riccardo's memorable self-sacrifice.

Where you have a Christ-figure, naturally, you often have a Passion Play. The word *passion* means struggle or suffering, and when we think of Christ's Passion we think of his two trials and death by crucifixion. Passion Plays were very popular in the later Middle Ages and they are still produced. Often we find them presented outdoors in the summer, to mobs of tourists, as in the Black Hills of South Dakota. Sometimes we find local churches staging Passion Plays annually, but generally they are beyond the resources of a single congregation.

In a narrow sense, only those plays involving Jesus Christ as a character would be Passion Plays. In a broader sense, any play which lifts up a suffering Christian hero or heroine would be one—Joan of Arc, for example, or Riccardo in *The Deputy*. Perhaps the best known of the modern Passion Plays are the musicals, *Jesus Christ Superstar* and *Godspell*, which have been staged professionally with performances running into the hundreds.

My preference between the two is *Godspell*. I believe it to be less cynical and more authentic in its portrayal of the gospel and the Christian faith than *Superstar*; also, I like its delightfully varied music better. *Godspell* has a more hopeful ending than *Superstar* but neither play actually depicts the resurrection. In Michael Ballard's production of *Godspell* at Eastern College he wanted a strong resurrection, so at the conclusion—after Jesus is lifted and carried down the aisle to the song, "Long Live God," he was directed to jump down from the arms of his "pallbearers" and bounce up the aisle and onto the stage once more to lead the audience in singing "Day by Day."

Godspell has an affinity with the medieval mysteries: It opens with an "I am God" speech, it engages the audience in lively interaction, and it uses a number of modern comic routines. Some people have scorned *Godspell*, with its vaudevillian humor, music hall-circus atmosphere, and flamboyant costuming and stage business. But this play that was first a student production inspired by Harvey Cox's *Feast of Fools* became a resounding box office success when it appeared off-Broadway in the seventies; more importantly, it has had a powerful spiritual effect on many lives. Scores of Christians have delighted in the play's exuberant joy, finding it not improper to have Jesus portrayed as a clown character in a Superman shirt. *Godspell's* Jesus is not a complete portrayal of our Lord, nor is it meant to be, but the sheer exuberance of the clown motif conveys the "abundant life" that Jesus said he had brought for us. A *Life* theatre critic wrote: "The show's power is not that it preaches Christian doctrine, but that it actually creates a festive, spontaneous, love-thy-neighbor mood. The sermon is not so much stated as demonstrated, and it is the clown-Christ who leads the demonstration."

At Eastern College we used an audience feedback sheet to record people's reactions to *Godspell*. To the question, "Was the play true to your understanding of the story of Jesus?" ninety-one out of ninety-four viewers said "Yes." However, twenty out of ninety-eight respondents said "Yes" to the question, "Was any part of the gospel distorted or was anything significant left out?" Clearly, *Godspell* is not the *whole gospel*; but then, what is, except the gospels?

Many of our viewers indicated on our survey that their faith had been "reinforced or enhanced" by the performance. A few were upset. One wrote, "the character of Jesus wasn't that of the Christ but of a clownish preacher who was 'one of the boys.'

Jesus' special nature of being the way back to God wasn't sufficiently presented." But others said: "Excellent—showed a compassionate Christ." "The meaning of the Gospel was significant." "When actors came into the audience to sing, "Light of the World," one could sense the power of what that meant!" Etc.

In its entirety, *Godspell* is a huge undertaking for a congregation, and certainly for the typical youth group. But the show may be done in pieces, or singers and musicians may be assembled to present the songs without doing the stage business. And of course there are less ambitious musicals like Helen Kromer's popular *For Heaven's Sake* and the recent *Cotton Patch Gospel*, as well as a readers' theatre piece with folk music, Kurtz' *A Matter of Death and Life*, shorter and easier to stage, yet profound.

Cotton Patch Gospel, with original music by Harry Chapin, is a marvelous piece. The book was adapted by Tom Key and Russell Treyz from the "Cotton Patch" translations of Matthew and John by the late Clarence Jordan, a Bible scholar and farmer who pioneered in Southern race relations by establishing Koinonia, an interracial Christian community in Georgia. Like Jordan's translations of scripture, *Cotton Patch Gospel* contemporizes the Christ-story in Chapin's scintillating bluegrass music and rural down-home Southern dialogue, beginning with Christ's birth in Gainesville! The play may be done by a cast of one actor and four musicians—as it was toured professionally—or by an expanded cast. The music lacks the rich variety of that in *Godspell*, and the show as a whole is somewhat less creative, but it has an earthy animation and an infectious gaiety that makes it fine theatre and acceptable theology—and it comes complete with a resurrection!

Godspell and *Cotton Patch Gospel* are some of the best theatre that Christians can offer. Plays like these, putting the Christ-story in a circus locale or, in the case of the movie version of *Godspell*, a junkyard and a wharf, public fountains, and the streets of New York—or, in the case of *Cotton Patch Gospel*, the rural South— help us translate the gospel into our time and our lives. Indeed, they help us know what it is to be a disciple of Christ in the latter twentieth century.

Oberammergau

Any discussion of biblical plays, or Passions, would be incomplete without mention of the granddaddy of them all, the Oberammergau Passion Play.

Oberammergau is a tiny German village of 4,500, sixty miles south of Munich. In 1633 a plague swept through the town, killing 350 of its 1,600 inhabitants. The town fathers decided to bargain with God; if the plague ended, they would stage a dramatic representation of the suffering and death of Jesus Christ every ten years. The plague ended, and the grateful citizens fulfilled their vow. Except for the interruption of two wars, they have given a performance every ten years, with a special one added in 1984 to mark the 350th anniversary of the play's first showing.

Although the Oberammergau play enjoys worldwide renown, the production is done by non-professionals. The 1,000 actors come from the 4,500 villagers, as do the 500 persons on the production staff. The leading roles are coveted by the villagers, who must either have been born in Oberammergau or have lived there twenty years to be eligible. The actors are selected by reputation and character more than for their acting talent. The woman playing Mary must be a virgin and be under thirty-five. All other women in the play must be married. Men also must have excellent reputations to land a leading role. In the 1980 production, a local plumber played Judas and a dentist's son Jesus.

The play consists of fourteen acts and sixty scenes and costs about $250,000 to produce. It is a seven-hour performance, running from 9:00 a.m. to 5:00 p.m., with a long lunch break. Over the years a number of changes have been made in the original text, to give the play more relevance, clear up obscurities, and eliminate anti-Semitic references. Another development, bringing the play closer to the English cycles, was the insertion of twenty-five Old Testament tableaus, each prefiguring some aspect of Christ's Passion.

The Passion itself, according to witnesses, is portrayed with great reverence by actors who seem totally immersed in their roles. The actor playing Jesus has a huge part—he has to memorize over 7,000 words—and he endures a physically draining ordeal of twenty-two minutes on the cross, something he prepares for months in advance by engaging in exercises designed to develop physical stamina.

Some viewers find the Oberammergau Passion undramatic and dull; it is long, and the lines are spoken in German, of course. Critics have called it a "movie cast without cameras and film," or "Super-Lent." But most Christian observers find it absorbing, a deeply moving faith experience. For many Christians, this Passion presented by "amateurs" provides a stronger spiritual lift, an authentic faith-experience, than anything to come out of Broadway. Carol Thiessen, writing a review for *Christianity Today* (9/21/84) concluded,

> To the Christian, it is not mere drama, it is a reenactment. And observing it thus, it is all but impossible to walk out of the huge hall unmoved.
>
> The importance the hardy residents of Oberammergau place on their vows and commitments to God serves as an ongoing example. Here, in a tiny village in Western Germany, God is real. And it is that reality that powers one of the world's most famous theatres.

So much for "amateur" productions. The clear line between amateur and professional productions is simply that the amateur isn't paid for his or her work—at least not in material goods! But often the distinction is fuzzy in terms of quality, which is why I prefer to use the term *nonprofessional*, not "amateur."

When people with some basic talent are devoted to a display of the Word through theatre, marvelous things happen! In attending five productions of *Godspell*, I have found the three nonprofessional ones warmer, richer, and more enjoyable than the two commercial productions I witnessed.

That may have something to do with the fact that a good dose of spiritual commitment makes up for a fair amount of inexperience. Talent and training are important; but Christians can act out the gospel brilliantly with minimal talent—honed in rehearsal to a fine edge of performance polish—thanks to the indwelling, enabling, encouraging divine spirit.

4

Updating the Scene

It is safe to say that nowhere and at no time since the Middle Ages has more Christian theatre been produced than in America today, in Protestant and Catholic parishes, by professional touring groups, and in church-related and independent Christian colleges.

Interestingly, the Mormons were the first American religious community to make much use of drama. MacGowen credits them with establishing the first community theatre in America at Nauvoo, Illinois, in 1843.[1] Brigham Young said, "The stage can be made to aid the pulpit in impressing upon the minds of the community an enlightened sense of a virtuous life." The Mormons built a fine theatre at Salt Lake City in 1862 that became a favorite playhouse for itinerant actors of the late nineteenth century; and the Mormons themselves produced family-oriented drama, with an emphasis on righteous living.

The Mormon Church is organized in wards (a small area including about five hundred members) and stakes (larger regions of four or more wards). Wards often produce original plays or "Road Shows," and stakes occasionally produce larger productions, pageants or musicals. Although many of their productions are standard plays and musicals, some are ostensibly religious, including *Stone Tables*, a serious musical on the life of Moses, and *Heubener*, the story of a German Mormon who was beheaded for resisting Adolf Hitler during World War II.

Certainly the mainstream Protestant churches dabbled in drama during the late nineteenth century, particularly in their new Sunday School programs, but it was in the early twentieth century that significant advances were made. The Drama League of America, founded in 1911, tried to promote interest in drama as a teaching tool in the Protestant communions. Many embraced the idea, the term "religious drama" assumed currency, and the League conducted religious drama contests and secured a publisher to print its best plays.

Other ecumenical ventures followed. In 1924 the Federal Council of Churches created a Committee on Religous Drama; later, Friendship Press, related to the National Council today, published a number of discussion plays designed to increase mission awareness (in the broader sense of "mission"). In 1949 the Religious Drama Workshop of the National Council of Churches was formed at the American Baptist Assembly at Green Lake, Wisconsin, under the tutelage of Amy Loomis, who had distinguished herself in a drama ministry at the Fountain Street Baptist Church in Grand Rapids, Michigan. Denominations began to add drama workshops to their summer conference schedules.

Meanwhile, the Chicago Theological Seminary had in 1940 surveyed 354 churches, each with a membership of 300 or more, sampling six denominations in nine geographical areas. Almost 90 percent reported using drama in their regular programs, and in 1940 had presented an average of 2.7 plays per church. Clearly, the renaissance in religious drama did not begin in America in the seventies and eighties, as we might like to think. But the Chicago Seminary survey included only sizable churches. My guess is that the larger churches are still using drama today; but, in addition, many more of the smaller congregations are bringing drama into their programs.

Pageantry and spectacle gained in popularity during the 1920s. *The Wayfarer* opened on July 20, 1919, as part of a Methodist Centenary Missionary Exposition held at the Ohio State Fairgrounds. The pageant consisted of nine episodes in three parts, "The Captivity," "The Christ," and "The Conquest." This was an elaborate morality play in which the Wayfarer, an Everyman-type, moved through the revelation of God's plan of salvation, from despair to faith. Another popular pageant, *The Pilgrimage Play*, emerged in Southern California in 1920. This portrayal of the life and ministry of Jesus was produced in a new outdoor theatre near the property that is now the Hollywood

Bowl. The play was given almost every summer until 1961, with financial support from the Department of Parks and Recreation of Los Angeles County. In 1961 the state Attorney General declared it illegal to use public funds to support religious productions, and the pageant's demise followed.

Other Passion Plays developed elsewhere, with the Black Hills Passion Play, originating in 1932, as one of the pioneers. That play is still running, as well as others, including the Smoky Mountain Passion Play in Tennessee, the Zion Passion Play in Illinois, and the Great Passion Play in Arkansas. Sometimes pageants become controversial and make news. In March of 1983, four performances of the thirteenth century Carmina Burana Passion Play, given at the Cloisters, New York City, drew angry protests from the Anti-Defamation League of B'nai B'rith: many contended the production was patently anti-Semitic. And a musical rendition of the life of Christ, *Worthy Is the Lamb*, which a producer wanted to stage as outdoor theatre on a mesa near Granbury, Texas, drew fire from local residents in 1984. It became a hot issue in the region, with the play's proponents citing both Christian witness and possible financial benefits to the community as reasons for producing the play at Commanche Peak, a sacred area for the local Indians. The play's detractors called the plans a desecration of a scenic spot and unbridled commercialism. One objector wrote the local editor, "Somehow a Commanche carnival for Christ does not smack of divine inspiration."

British Developments

Let's jump the Atlantic for a moment. The development of British religious drama is worth examining in its own right, apart from any influence it has had on the American scene.

By 1922 there was room for improvement. During the early twentieth century, church drama historian Murray Roston tells us, religious drama was typified by Miss A.M. Buckton's extremely popular Christmas pageant, *Eager Heart*:

> Young Eager Heart, resisting the blandishments of Eager Fame and Eager Sense while awaiting the coming of the King, hears a knock at the door. She finds a poor family seeking shelter and ... generously invites them in and offers them the food she has so carefully prepared for her royal guest. The poor family is, of course, suddenly transformed into the Holy Family of the nativ-

ity, and the pageant concludes with the pointed question to the audience: "Is *your* hearth ready?"[2]

Public interest in the pageant waned by 1922, Roston says, and by 1928 the church—if not the public—was ready for a more profound Christian theatre. The prime mover was the Dean of Canterbury, George K.A. Bell, who in 1928 commissioned the poet John Masefield to write a play for performance on the steps of Canterbury Cathedral.

This was Masefield's *The Coming of Christ*, a rather formal biblical work. As Roston argues, "characters introducing themselves 'I am a shepherd who keeps fold . . .' could scarcely stimulate an audience bred on Ibsen and Shaw."[3] But the eminent Masefield focused interest on the annual Canterbury festival, and other distinguished authors wrote works expressly for it in the ensuing years; Charles Williams, Dorothy Sayers, and Christopher Fry were among those whose first attempts at religious drama were produced at Canterbury, and in 1935 the most eminent of all Canterbury dramas was given, T. S. Eliot's *Murder in the Cathedral*. This play was tailored for Canterbury like no other, since it concerned the famous Archbishop Thomas Becket, who had been assassinated at the Cathedral by knights associated with King Henry II. The play's verse is haunting and evocative and appropriately elevates a Christian hero, affirming the grandeur of a life well lived and offered willingly to God.

The works performed at Canterbury inspired the founding of the Religious Drama Society of Great Britain in 1929, which encouraged new plays and writers, some of whose works became popular with American audiences—R.H. Ward and P.W. Turner being the most obvious candidates. Incidentally, one of the founders of the Society was the explorer, Sir Francis Younghusband, who in his travels overseas had noticed that Communists were using drama successfully to spread their gospel among the Asian masses. Younghusband felt that Christians should promote their faith at least as vigorously as the Communists were promoting theirs, and that drama would become a significant vehicle.

British drama didn't cease with World War II. Instead, a significant event happened with the production of an elaborate radio cycle on the life of Christ, Dorothy Sayers' *The Man Born to Be King*. These twelve plays, sanctioned by the Church of England, were to be written in a vigorous realism. Instead of using the Authorized Version, Sayers chose to translate from the original Greek into the vernacular. This was a huge task: Sayers said after finishing her last script that she had "worn out one Greek New Testament and amassed a considerable theological library." But she wanted to reduce the distance between the biblical figures and events and the present day, avoiding "that stained-glass-window decorum with which the tale is usually presented to us," in which "the characters are not men and women: they are all 'sacred personages', standing about in symbolic attitudes, and self-consciously awaiting the fulfillment of prophecies."[4]

In her introduction to the published version of *The Man Born to Be King*, Sayers explains that she was working for a realism that would shock people, particularly in reference to Christ's execution—for they ought to be shocked by it!

> If that does not shock them, nothing can. If the mere representation of it has an air of irreverence, what is to be said about the deed? It is curious that people who are filled with horrified indignation whenever a cat kills a sparrow can hear that story of the killing of God told Sunday after Sunday and not experience any shock at all.[5]

Although announcement of the forthcoming BBC series produced howls of "blasphemy," "irreverent!" and "vulgar!" from conservative critics, the radio plays were given during 1942 and 1943, as Great Britain fought for its life against the Axis powers. Listeners were not unanimously favorable; in fact, some regarded these plays as related to setbacks in the war—one thought them responsible for the fall of Singapore! But the BBC collected files of grateful letters from its listeners whose faith was increased during those desperate years by the pungent, colloquial dialogue and the winsome, more human Jesus of *The Man Born to Be King*.

With characteristic foresight, the Religious Drama Society of Great Britain in 1956 commissioned Orlin Corey to develop a play for a summer tour of English churches. Actually, the play was birthed at Georgetown College in Kentucky: It was Orlin and Irene Corey's adaptation of *The Book of Job*.

The popularity of this production has been phenomenal. The production played three years off-Broadway, has toured four continents, was featured at the Brussels World's Fair in 1958, was filmed in Latin America and shown on the BBC in England, and has moved thousands of viewers every summer where it has played at the Pine Mountain State Park, Pineville, Kentucky, since 1959. With hundreds of performances, the play's "run" has far exceeded all but the most popular Broadway shows of the past thirty years.

The Book of Job is entirely derived from the Old Testament book. Orlin Corey describes it as "an arrangement of the ancient argument . . . derived from the example of Aaeschylus' *Prometheus Bound*, who utilized chorus as counterpoint to the protagonist. In the visual and vocal mosaic we sought an utterance appropriate to the music and message of what may be the oldest story in the Bible."[6] The costuming and makeup are lavish and spectacular: Irene Corey has designed a mosaic makeup effect for the actors' faces, with the costuming coordinated. The effect is to eternalize the story of Job, depicting it as ancient yet timeless. Corey's *Job* is a striking piece of biblical theatre: the production richly deserves its fame.

Probably nothing has moved British Christians more since World War II than the remarkable musical play, *Ride! Ride!*[7] One hundred two thousand people saw this dramatic portrayal of John Wesley between March 2 and July 24, 1976, alone. The show played a week in each of eleven cities, followed by an eleven-week run in London's West End, at the Westminster Theatre. The *Guardian* critic wrote, "in his time John Wesley would have regarded anything to do with the theatre as the work of the devil. But he would approve of the way his church is using the medium." And the BBC commentator: "I have a strong suspicion that John Wesley would applaud the use of one of the country's major theatres to present something of the Christian faith because, make no mistake, that is what *Ride! Ride!* is all about."

Alan Thornhill, the author of the book and lyrics, is a distinguished playwright with many London successes. Thornhill writes of the origin of *Ride! Ride!*: "When Dr. Maldwyn Edwards, the notable Methodist preacher and Wesley scholar, saw my play, *Mr. Wilberforce, MP*, he said, 'Now you must write a play about Wesley.'" Thornhill asked Edwards to provide him with a story about "one of Wesley's innumerable adventures with people."[8] Anecdotes, as we know, are the basic stuff of biographical drama. Edwards produced the story of Martha Thompson, a Lancashire girl who ran off to London to seek adventure, who became converted by Wesley, and consequently was thrown into

Bedlam (prison) by her master. "How John Wesley rescued her from Bedlam, and personally escorted her, riding pillion behind him, back to her family in Preston, is as exciting and moving a story as you can find."

Ride! Ride! was first produced by an amateur group and given at the British Methodist conference at Newcastle in 1973. The conference felt it should be presented in every Methodist district of the United Kingdom "as an effective means of evangelism." That task seemed too big for an amateur company so a professional one, Aldersgate Productions, Ltd., was formed. With a great deal of volunteer labor and financed entirely by private donations and trusts, *Ride! Ride!* was produced with twenty-three actors, six musicians, and six technicians. Wesley's twin focus on personal evangelism and social reform, combined with an amazing vitality in acting and music, affected spectators deeply. Comments included, "It made me rethink my whole life," "It made me face the bitterness I had in my heart and decide to be different," and "I will never be the same again!"

Since then *Ride! Ride!* has enjoyed many successful productions in the United States and New Zealand as well as the United Kingdom, and Aldersgate has gone on to produce other significant works, including an adaptation of C. S. Lewis' *The Lion, the Witch, and the Wardrobe*, which enjoyed its second national British tour in 1986. Aldersgate celebrated its tenth anniversary in March, 1986, and announced plans to produce a second dramatic adaptation from the Narnia series, *The Voyage of the Dawn Treader*. Also, in September of 1986, Aldersgate would incorporate performers from several theatre companies to tour the play *Zeal*, based on the experiences of the Soviet dissident, Sergei Kourdakov.

American Developments

Christian touring groups developed in America as well, with the Wesley Players being pioneers. They were founded in 1924 as a national organization with chapters on several campuses. The British post-war troupe, The Pilgrim Players, may have spurred interest here.

Encouraged by Methodist Bishop Gerald Kennedy, eight Hollywood actors founded the Bishops Company in 1952. This professional troupe toured until 1968 with as many as five acting units in the field, generally using adaptations of Christian classics such as C. S. Lewis' *Screwtape Letters* and *The Great Divorce.* They used a barestage style with each unit having several plays in its repertory.

In 1954, Albert and Bertha Johnson were asked by the president of Redlands University to form a mobile unit that could travel as a "poor theatre," without benefit of properties or scenery— and to perform in modern dress. The result was the Redlands Drama Trio, a unit of three actors, two men and one woman. Albert Johnson wrote some ten plays for his Trios, with the first, *Roger Williams and Mary*, being presented at the First Baptist Church of Los Angeles in 1954. The Redlands Trio became nationally known in a short time. It is no longer active, but it has been succeeded by numerous college theatre troupes, some of which tour widely; others perform only in a limited region around the college.

Colleges and seminaries began to offer coursework in religious drama in the fifties and sixties. Led by Robert Seaver and fostered by a grant from the Rockefeller Foundation in 1955, Union Seminary in New York developed a strong drama program. Alfred Edyvean pioneered a religious theatre program at Christian Theological Seminary in Indianapolis; similarly, Harold Ehrensperger at Boston University. More recently a journal, *Religious Theatre*, was created to publish original works, with such distinguished men as Tom Driver and Warren Kliewer being editorially involved. During the seventies the Religious Drama Project of the American Theatre Association, spearheaded by Dale Rott of Bethel College (St. Paul, Minnesota) and Norman Fedder of Kansas State University (Manhattan, Kansas) began an ongoing newsletter, *Religion and Theatre*,[9] encouraged original works, and offered a lending library of playscripts. The Ecumenical Council for Drama and the Arts (ECDA), with Wilma Ringstrom as guiding light, has been active during the period in sponsoring workshops, and with other projects designed to improve the state of religious drama.

In Minneapolis, meanwhile, the Christian Theatre Artists Guild was founded in the mid-seventies as an umbrella organization. Its purpose was to network groups across the country, catalogue resource persons in Christian drama and the media, and provide encouragement for aspiring Christian playwrights. The organization conducted an annual playwrighting contest and published a *Theatrical Resource Guide* listing troupes, art organizations, and contact agencies. CTAG folded shortly after the *Guide*'s publication in 1979, having made a real contribution to the American Christian arts scene. Telly Olsen, former CTAG president, has since begun a Creative Gift Foundation designed to provide significant grants to Christian arts projects. The Foundation had assets of $200,000 by the end of 1985 and during that year had made grants totaling $10,000.

The enormous success of *Godspell* has certainly inspired artists working from a Christian perspective, and has stimulated church dramatic activity. Networking has spread with, for example, the publication of a newsletter, *Christian Drama*,[10] by Nonna Childress Dalan of Evangel College in Springfield, Missouri. Professor Dalan writes, "In the eight years I have worked with *Christian Drama*, the number of requests for information and material, the number of new drama groups that are being formed, and the churches that have been appointing drama directors, has been growing steadily."

At least one major denomination, the Southern Baptist Convention, has a full-time national drama staff person. Other denominations follow, somewhat less ambitiously. Several publishers have been printing more religious drama; in addition to the major houses (Samuel French and Baker's, especially), Contemporary Drama Service, a relative newcomer, has been highly successful in generating a church drama market; recently, Pioneer Drama Service has decided to develop a religious component. And there are more recent newcomers, such as Lillenas. These are signs of a tremendous health, even a vigorous *growth* in religious drama—if not Christian theatre—in America. In the remainder of the chapter we'll look at what's happening in more detail, beginning with professional companies, then moving to educational institutions, churches, ecumenical ventures, and one major denomination.

Professionals

There is a thin line between nonprofessional and professional acting companies. Christians seldom make a substantial salary in doing theatre—often barely a living wage—and yet they may see their work as a ministry—their *vocation*—and be satisfied with arduous travel, difficult playing conditions, and hand-to-mouth or faith financing. Defining a *professional* as simply one who is more or less full-time in ministry, we have among us today several strong successors to the Bishops company. The most eminent (or at least the most durable) of these would seem to be the Covenant Players, the After Dinner Players, the Lamb's Players, and Taproot Theatre Company.

The Covenant Players[11] was founded in 1963 by Charles Tanner, who has written its entire repertory, which by 1986 included over 1,500 dramatic pieces—almost entirely short sketches or stingers, and longer one-act plays. The company was designed to present programs of works drawn from repertory, before both church and secular audiences. The latter include hospitals, civic groups, armed forces, fraternal organizations, and high schools. Generally, Tanner's plays have a pointed message or moral, often softened by humor, and the program is varied to reach the various audiences.

The Covenant Players have evolved into a far-flung organization with a worldwide dramatic ministry. As of January 1, 1986, the organization had 110 touring units in the field, with sixty of them in North America and Canada, and the others overseas—with over 500 people being employed. Acting units now perform not only in English, but in many other languages, including German, French, Danish, and Swahili!

A Covenant Players unit normally consists of four to five actors, but they have added teams doing three-act plays, calling for five to six players each. The organization exists to tour—there is no resident theatre—and a unit normally tours five months at a time. The actors perform on a bare stage with just a few chairs as props. The team leader explains the setting for each play, encouraging the audience to use its imagination, and after the play is finished the curtain line is followed by the leader's call of "Curtain!"

I have seen a number of Covenant Players units; although Tanner has written some clever material, he tends to sacrifice profundity for punch; most of the sketches are very brief, with thin characters, but they are pointed. The acting units vary a good deal in dramatic ability. Unhappily, there is only a two-week period of training for new actors before going on tour. Since this is a large operation with a good deal of turnover—actors come and go constantly—almost any candidate is accepted, whether or not he or she has any innate ability. Also, because of the enormous amount of material written by a single prolific author, the quality cannot be consistently high. Other companies,

75

being more discriminating as to actors and material, have an artistic advantage.

One of them is the After Dinner Players,[12] incorporated in 1967. I have seen the "A.D." Players perform only once, but I was quite impressed with the competence of the six-person team. They were very professional (in the sense of maintaining high artistic standards): The actors had strong, expressive voices, they did excellent mime and able characterization. The material was biblically based, with modern allusions, and with good humor. They used only six stools for the one-act, *Demi-tasse*, which consisted of headlines and other modern media stuff depicting salvation history through Jesus Christ. It was a lively, contemporized version of God's grand invasion of the world. The acting was precise, evocative, vivacious. The costuming was modern, with everyone wearing an unassuming blue outfit.

Jeanette Clift George is the talented founder and playwright of A.D. Players. "We called ourselves the After Dinner Players," she writes, "because we hoped to be fed prior to each performance!" Currently the company has twenty full-time members. They have organized a National Christian Drama Seminar and various workshops and classes in the Houston area. But their primary reason for existing is performance. There are touring units of four to six actors and a resident company which performs at the Grace Theatre in Houston, Texas. Five full-length productions plus special matinees are produced annually at this 212-seat theatre, which also houses offices, work rooms, and rehearsal space. These people are busy: On a March day two years ago, the A.D. Players played four shows in the Houston area, two shows in Tennessee, six shows on tour in Germany, and a fully produced play in Grace Theatre!

The Lamb's Players[13] was founded by the irrepressible Steve Terrell. In a letter dated March 26, 1975, and signed "Your Broken Legged Brother" (theatre buffs will follow that stage allusion), Terrell explained to me how the Lamb's Players began. He had first organized The King's Players at Biola College—which the Terrells themselves financed, since at that time "theatrical trappings" were suspect at Biola. Then Terrell moved to St. Paul, Minnesota, and Bethel College, "where I was given more freedom to develop evangelical Christian drama. Bethel awarded me an alumni grant in 1970 to research street theatre . . . I was frustrated with catching a few lost sinners as they wandered into a church. I wanted to get out into the marketplace."

76

During the summer of 1970, Steve and Else Terrell researched street theatre in Berkeley, California. Returning to Minnesota, Steve produced an original script, *The Hound of Everyman*, in the fall of 1970, and performances of *Hound* were given in Minnesota parks during the next summer. But Steve was unhappy with the weather: the Terrells moved to San Diego where the weather was propitious and theatre could be performed outdoors year-round. The troupe has grown there, and during the ensuing years work has been done in puppetry, mime, readers' theatre, and film ministries. I have seen a performance of readers' theatre by their touring group: It was a compiled script developed by Todd Lewis and Richard Parker, *Pardon Me, Christian, but Your Old Nature Is Showing*, and it was excellent.

Currently, in January, 1986, the Lamb's Players are retooling their street theatre emphasis. They are working hard at their prison ministry and their resident theatre, now the third largest year-round house in the San Diego area. More about the original Lamb's Players street theatre later!

The Taproot Theatre Company[14] has done extensive work in the Northwest. Scott L. Nolte, its Producing Artistic Director, has written to me that Taproot "began in response to the vision and dreams of some Christian actors, and to the unique needs of the Pacific Northwest. Seattle has the highest per capita dollar spent on theatre and movies in the country . . . and the lowest church attendance (only 5 percent attend any kind of church regularly). However, TTC has not seen itself as an 'evangelistic' theatre; rather, we are dedicated to preserving the integrity of Christian values and perspectives."

Taproot had a staff of nine by January 1, 1986, seven of which were full-time. It is primarily a touring theatre with a repertoire that has included George MacDonald's modern fairy tale, *The Light Princess*, a collection of American stories and folk music under the title, *American Trinity, The Way of the Wolf*, adapted from Martin Bell's animal fable, and Norman Dietz' *Old Ymir's Clay Pot*.

Also, Taproot has been extremely successful in generating discussion about chemical and drug abuse with its presentation of Gillette Elvgren's *I Am the Brother of Dragons*, the story of a teenager and his family. "Razz-ma-tazz theatrics, vaudeville routines, and 'rapping' style music communicate the harsh realities of chemical dependency," according to the brochure. Scott Nolte says, "We hope and pray that the Theatre's magical ability to evoke emotion and thought will call some back from the abyss."

Other professionals doing Christian theatre include the Jeremiah People (largely music, but doing some drama—they have published a number of *Sketch Books*),[15] and the Lampost Theatre Company, an outreach arm of the Iowa Christian Theatre.[16]

The name "Lampost" is derived from Matthew 5:15: "Nor do men light a lamp and put it under a bushel, but on a stand, and it gives light to all in the house." Lampost has ministered in churches, prisons, and coffeehouses, as well as to many high school audiences. Their fall 1985 itinerary had them traveling beyond the midwest to California. This troupe uses music with some of their sketches, and with a strong emphasis on mime. Sue Stanley writes of her apprehension facing a performance at an Ohio state prison:

> As we went inside the walls, doors slammed insensitively shut behind me. We walked briskly down a long hall and entered a tiny gymnasium. In the middle of the gym was a tiny stage. Soon three hundred men were filing in and they sat waiting for what we came to share. I looked around for guards and saw only two or three, none of which seemed to be alert. Didn't they know I was a girl among three hundred salvages?
>
> As our program neared the end we invited men to come and pray to receive Jesus into their hearts. The next thing I knew these "salvages" were holding hands with me in a circle praying to Jesus for a new life.

I don't know whether "salvages" was a misprint in the Lampost newsletter, but I have kept it in. "Convicts" may seem to be "savages" to those who fear them, but to those who reach them with the gospel they are indeed *salvages*, those salvaged or rescued through Christ and the work of his people.

Colleges and Seminaries

Historically, three seminaries have perhaps been the strongest in drama: Chicago Theological Seminary, Union Seminary in New York, and Christian Theological Seminary in Indianapolis; but many others have become involved. The list would include the Pacific School of Religion in Berkeley, California; and the School of Theology at Claremont, California, where quite recently, a musical play highlighting the early history of the Disciples of Christ has been presented. Playscripts and even a video-tape of the production are available from the Disciples Seminary Foundation. Also, there are new communications programs at certain Southern Baptist seminaries, notably Southwestern, in Fort Worth, Texas, which has over two hundred communications majors; some coursework in drama is included in the program.

Christian theatre has spread more widely among colleges, including the more conservative Christian schools where, in the past, theatre of any kind has been suspect. Probably Biola College and Bethel (Minnesota) are good examples. In February, 1984, M. James Young of Wheaton reported on a survey of Christian college theatre programs, to which eighteen colleges responded.[17]

Professor Young found that the eighteen respondents all did some theatre. (Of course, most of those who don't do theatre won't respond.) Seven of the eighteen have touring groups performing in churches. These include Transformed! (Eastern College), The Crossroads Theatre Company (Grove City), Genesis Players (Judson), and Disciples in Drama (Olivet Nazarene College).

Most of the respondents indicated that they had access to an auditorium, but eleven of the eighteen said they had to share the premises with others, competing for rehearsal time. Many had to be content with classrooms, old gyms, and "black boxes" for rehearsal space, and most complained of inadequate shop and storage areas.

Christian college directors will often modify or edit the language of a playscript, as well as discriminate in choosing scripts. Young's survey indicates that 44 percent of his sample say they omit profane language and 56 percent edit it severely to delete use of God's name; 38 percent omit obscene language and 62 percent edit it; 62 percent omit any smoking; only 6 percent omit drinking on the set but 50 percent say they "de-emphasize it," whatever that means.

Young asked his correspondents about their criteria for play selection, which he grouped into categories. The major criteria include: (1) moral outlook—are the play's values and action consistent with a Christian world-view? (2) academic value—what are its merits as drama and literature? (3) suitability for students—are there enough female roles? and (4) community appeal and commercial potential. The list of plays these colleges have done recently includes secular titles like *The Odd Couple, Indians,* and

She Stoops to Conquer, as well as musicals and melodramas and more ostensibly religious works. Although there was a widespread variety in the plays cited, *The Miracle Worker, The Fantastiks*, and *You Can't Take It with You* were mentioned more often than others.

Local Congregations

To add to my understanding of what's happening today, I mailed a questionnaire to about two hundred persons on four mailing lists—persons known to have done religious drama or who, because of their jobs, are likely to be involved in religious drama. The vast majority of the forty-one respondents were Christians "doing their thing" in a local congregation, both ministers and laity.

Churches report a wide variety of activities in chancel drama, dinner theatre, pageantry, educational plays, etc. Their philosophies differ too. One church took pride in reporting three annual productions: traditional Christmas and Easter plays, plus a spring comedy or musical to keep everyone happy. Another reported that it was much more fulfilling to maintain a continuing group doing regular plays and improvisations than to do just the seasonal dramas. And although my respondents were generally theatre buffs, some congregations may still be reluctant to present some of the more popular plays because of theological qualms. For example, Professor Dale Savidge reports that in selecting plays at Bob Jones University they look for "good dramatic quality and a reverence for Christ and respect for his deity (we wouldn't do *Godspell*)."

Some larger churches report doing major, spectacular productions. The Colonial Heights Baptist Church and Bellevue Baptist, of Kingsport and Memphis, Tennessee, respectively, have been doing "Living Pictures" productions. These are biblical pageants involving scripture, music, costumed biblical scenes, often in tableau, sophisticated lighting and special effects. They seem eminently successful: The Bellevue church *Messenger* reported that in 1982 the estimated number attending performances was twenty-one thousand, with 945 indicating on their decision cards that they had prayed to receive Jesus; in 1985 the twelve performances of "Living Pictures" found 1,614 persons praying to receive.

Stanley Miles, minister of music at the Colonial Heights Baptist Church, has compiled an extensive slide show, which is available at cost to help other congregations who want to get into the pageant ministry.[18] The script accompanying the slide show describes the technical side in great detail, down to the donkey used for the triumphal entry (⅛" plywood cutout), the palms (real ones from Florida, spray-painted green) and the archway (styrofoam). Costumes, props, scenery and lighting are all explained—little is left to the imagination.

Few churches can or will produce such big-scale drama: In fact, most of my correspondents indicated that they avoid drama that requires major scenic effects. Few of them have skilled professionals in the congregation to direct plays, although one had a Ph.D. in oral interpretation and another a poet-playwright to direct readers' theatre! I asked them what criteria they used in play selection, and found that the responses could be grouped this way: (1) must have a sound message and be theologically meaningful (2) should require limited or flexible staging (3) the material should have integrity, be artistic and (4) should meet the needs of the audience, players, and occasion.

There seems to be a lot of readers' theatre happening in the churches, and many are using mime and clowning along with standard plays. A few of the old classics (*Why the Chimes Rang, Family Portrait*) were mentioned, but most of my respondents seem to be doing new plays, some of them created by one or more persons in the congregation. A wide variety of titles were mentioned by this group, with just two plays listed more than once. Responses to the question, "What were your major difficulties?" varied according to the play, but typically there were either staging problems, problems working with a large cast, or problems related to commitment to rehearsals and scheduling.

Also, I asked my respondents to complete the statement, *The greatest benefit from doing Christian theatre is . . .* Here are some of the more vivid answers. The first four are from college directors, the rest from congregational dramatists:

". . . the opportunity to minister to the participants."

". . . to put Christ's message into a dramatic form to enhance its impact and usefulness for God's people."

". . . knowing that many people will be strengthened in their faith from witnessing a dramatized viewpoint which puts Christianity into practical and pragmatic application."

". . . presenting a well-worn, often overlooked message in a fresh new way, or presenting a new, revolutionary message in a comfortable old way."

". . . to bring the gospel to life."

". . . providing the opportunity for people to express their gifts in the corporate worship experience, and to allow and encourage stretching and growth among the performers."

". . . the family unit it builds with the cast and production crew."

". . . the opportunity it affords for generating meaningful dialogue."

". . . to introduce inexperienced people to the joys of drama and, secondly, to put 'legs' on scriptural/spiritual truth."

". . . watching the young people doing it go from 'Nope! I'm not going to do this!' to 'Wow! This was the best thing I've ever been involved in!'"

Cooperative Ventures

When Christian theatre needs a catalyst, or networking, or where it might not otherwise flourish, a healthy ecumenism may be the answer.

In some cases, Christians have developed regional or area associations of dramatists to encourage and promote or exchange playscripts and productions. Take Washington, D.C., for example, where in the late seventies and early eighties folks created an ecumenical drama steering committee for the greater Washington area, a newsletter, *Drama Dreamers*, which reported on the various local church drama groups—like the Heritage Players, the Parson's Players, Side Door Players and Potter's House Players—and an annual religious drama festival with live performers and workshops taught by eminent people in the field. This network seems to have broken down as of January, 1986, although several local groups continue.

Ecumenism also functions when local congregations decide to prepare productions to exchange with each other. In one city four churches created a drama circuit. Players in each church prepared their dramas, producing them first in their own churches and then taking them on succeeding Sunday evenings to the others. Each group had the advantage of four different audiences, justifying the immense time and energy put into a production and providing a learning experience for all. There was the added incentive of friendly competition, leading perhaps to the performance of somewhat more difficult plays, or at least to a kind of "quality control" that might otherwise be absent. These advantages seem to outweigh the possible prideful, "We can do it better than you!" attitude that may surface.

A third ecumenical approach would be the independent regional troupe. The King's Players of the Philadelphia area began as individuals from several churches shared time and interest to produce quality plays that would be offered to churches in the region. Rehearsing in various places, we developed a significant ministry during our seventeen years during which we gave over two hundred performances of fourteen plays. This was, you understand, a part-time ministry, an avocation for all of us. Around the country, similar companies surface and disappear as time goes on.

There is a fourth approach to doing ecumenical drama: persuade your "secular" community theatre group to produce one or more religious dramas. Michael Dixon, who edits youth materials for the Christian Board of Publication, reports that his community theatre annually produces a Lenten play and presents it in three or four churches. One has to be sensitive to Jews and agnostics in the community theatre network, but where there is a spiritually homogeneous community theatre, this would work well.

Southern Baptist Activity

By means of programming at the national level, or through publications, several of the major denominations encourage drama. Some have made good use of drama at national meetings to highlight doctrine or church history. For example, I wrote three historical plays to celebrate the 150th Anniversary of the American Baptist Home Mission Societies, which were given at the Biennial of American Baptist Churches in San Juan, Puerto Rico in 1981. And several denominations have developed national and regional workshops and seminars in drama. But none of the major Protestant communions seems to be using drama as extensively as Southern Baptists.

Of course, the Southern Baptist Convention, the nation's largest Protestant group, has significant resources. Many of these resources are devoted to church recreation programming, and drama is a part of that ministry. Southern Baptists hold national and regional recreation labs, in which workshops in different phases of drama, clowning, and puppetry are taught, and often state conventions hold religious drama festivals and workshops. I'm quoting from a letter I received from Everett Robertson, Drama Specialist on the national staff of the Southern Baptist Convention:

There is considerable evidence of steadily increasing interest in religious drama among Southern Baptists. This interest is being precipitated by changing communication patterns in our society and the great success of churches in using drama and related areas in many aspects of ministry . . . Our National Clowning Seminar has doubled in attendance. Many of our state festivals have very, very large crowds. Recently in Tennessee we had eight hundred at a state festival workshop. Other states have also had large crowds . . . composed of large numbers of adults (in addition to youth groups). For example, this fall the North Carolina Festival had over two hundred fifty people present and over seventy churches were represented.

It is certainly safe to say that over 50 percent of Southern Baptist churches utilize drama within a given year. And when one considers puppetry, clowning, and mime, that number would increase.

To select one area that is gaining in popularity would be difficult. Obviously, clowning has become more popular in recent years; however, there has been continual and regular growth in puppetry. . . . Perhaps the area of greatest growth is the production of pageants. Many of the larger churches in our denomination now produce one or two major pageants a year. . . . Even the state conventions are using pageants to give historical basis for present conditions and future growth.

I do not keep a list of all the local churches that have such groups, but it is safe to say that we have several hundred that have drama/clowning groups that regularly tour doing performances. We have several colleges that have touring groups. We also have some state conventions like the Kentucky Baptist Convention that has a special drama touring group each summer. (Robertson mentions two other states and two seminaries that often tour.) I can definitely say that the interest and continuing growth in drama is much larger than most Baptist leaders realize.

I do know that there has been phenomenal sales of some of our materials. (Mr. Robertson has edited several anthologies of drama for worship, monologues, etc., for Convention Press, and has written an excellent primer, *Introduction to Church Drama.*)[19] For example, the new clown ministry book which has been out a little over a year sold out the first printing of 5,000 in a three-month period. . . .[20] Certainly, that would indicate considerable interest in clowning and widespread use not only in Baptist circles but other denominations as well.

Although Southern Baptists are unique, considerable dramatic interest exists in many denominations. Christian theatre is alive and prospering!

This accelerating interest may be related to the growing awareness of the arts nationally. A Harris Poll taken in 1984 found that 67 percent of those surveyed reported they attend live theatre, up from 53 percent in 1975. Despite the lure of television soap operas and other, more exciting, electronic media fare, many Americans are attending live theatre—and the numbers are increasing.

Churches need to keep pace with this growing American exposure to the arts. Christians must take advantage of this interest, not in order to "outsell" motion pictures and television; but to utilize a medium that's widely enjoyed to promote spiritual and prophetic ideas. With theatre's help we can offer a different world view; we Christians provide an alternative frame of reference in a world reeking with despair and disillusionment, greed, materialism, and runaway technology.

5

Worship and Theatre: Varieties Thereof

"Let Us All Become Fools for Christ's Sake!" the Sunday bulletin proclaimed. As we entered the sanctuary we were greeted by gaily clad figures with white smiling faces and red bulbous noses. The ushers were clowns, the worship leaders were clowns, and clowns preached the sermon. It was a festive morning, a celebration of joy in living the life of faith, that Sunday when clowns led worship.

The liturgy contained the usual elements. Signs were displayed to announce each section: "Invocation," "Hymn of Praise," etc. Clowns are silent, so mime was the main vehicle. During the period of Absolution "Just As I Am" was played on the organ, with clowns being called forward to conversion: One clown whose eyes were covered had his vision restored, an earmuffed clown had his hearing impediment removed, and a clown in chains was freed from bondage . . . a dramatic message in song and mime. Later, the sermon was a modern parable of the good Samaritan.

Communion, too, was administered by clowns: One held bread and another the chalice as the worshipers filed by the table; the third clown bestowed a red spot on each worshiper's right cheek—the mark of the Christian clown. Another clown gave us a hug, another handed each of us a balloon, then back to our pews we went. Through it all, three trinitarian balloons flew high overhead in the rafters. After the benediction the clowns led us out onto the front lawn—where traffic pours by on a major highway—to release balloons.

This is one example of liturgical theatre, or, if you will, dramatized liturgy. It was upbeat and involving and helped us focus on the positive aspects of discipleship, the healing that happens and the grace and joy we feel when God is working in the world through us. God in clown costume, worship in whiteface . . . we were ministered to, and being led to minister.

Defining Worship

By now, we think we know what drama is, but . . . what is worship? Harry Emerson Fosdick described worship as "being carried out of oneself by something higher than oneself, to which one gives oneself." A rich statement, but too broad to define exactly what happens in the Protestant or Catholic liturgy on a Sunday morning or evening. Someone suggested that worship is "communication between God and man, initiated by man, which gives evidence of man's reverence for God"; but even apart from its biased language, the definition lacks something. So does the suggestion of an Episcopalian friend that "worship is the art form of the church," although it has a nice feel to it.

Worship is a two-way street. It provides opportunity for two-way communication. Humans are trying to reach up to God through prayer, confession, and commitment; and God is trying to reach us, his message given in the various forms the Word takes including, but not exclusively, the sermon. "Church drama," Olov Hartman writes, "is art in the service of a message . . . its distinctive aim is to proclaim God's word to the congregation and to express the congregation's intercessions before God."[1]

In one sense, worship is a rehearsal. As the Quakers used to say, "Service begins when the worship ends;" and some churches have on their bulletins, "Enter to worship. Depart to serve." If our real mission as disciples of Christ is to the world, the worshiping congregation becomes a support team and Sunday worship is a launching pad for apostles, a rehearsal for what we are to do elsewhere: We the people of God are rehearsing the gospel of love that we have to act out in the world!

The Dramatic Elements of Worship

Worship is inherently dramatic. The communion or Eucharist, by restaging an event in Christ's ministry, is an *acting out*, a dramatic ritual. Baptism too becomes dramatic, invested with meaning from its original context and the injunction to "go therefore and make disciples of all nations, baptizing them in the name of the Father and of the Son and of the Holy Spirit" (Matthew 28:19). But the worship service or liturgy as a whole is dramatic in itself to the extent that it gathers intensity, probes and explores conflict, and builds to a climax of commitment. The conflict in general is between good and evil, the base and the holy, God and the devil, elaborated through prayer, litanies, scripture reading, and sermon. The ultimate call to commitment implies or requires a "yes" response by the worshiping congregation—a *yes* to the divine demand to turn from evil and do good; further, we are called to a vocation, called to fulfill a ministry in and for the world.

The climax of the liturgy is not always the homily, as many believe; rather, the critical moment—symbolized in many cases by the taking of an offering—occurs whenever the worshiping congregation is invited to commit or recommit themselves to whatever the Word has challenged them to do that day. Some services fail in that they lack that important call to commitment.

Soren Kierkegaard said years ago that we have the wrong ideas about worship, and he used an analogy from theatre. At that time the Norwegian stage had a prompter for every performance who was placed in the wings or situated in a box or pit below the apron of the stage. (Today, aside from rehearsals, few directors use a prompter.) The prompter would whisper lines to actors at awkward moments.

So who is the prompter in worship, and who are the actors and spectators? Kierkegaard suggested that in worship:

WE THINK THAT . . .	WHEN ACTUALLY . . .
God is the prompter	The minister is the prompter
The minister is the actor	Worshipers are the actors
Worshipers are the audience	God is the audience[2]

A correspondent, Richard F. Crompton, associate pastor of the First Baptist Church of Colorado Springs, writes, "Each person is, after all, a performer before God. My role is to be a prompter both in worship and in the everyday life of the people God has entrusted to me."

So in worship we act out our praise, thanksgiving, and joy— and rehearse what it means to love as God loves. Perhaps the most dramatic worship is that in which the congregation is participating most fully. Sometimes the congregation is carried beyond its usual rather passive bump-on-a-pew role to a more physically involving one. At an Episcopal church near me, for example, there is an annual Palm Sunday service in which the total Passion narrative is used—printed in parts in the bulletin—and the roles of Narrator, Jesus, Disciples, Caiaphas, Pilate, etc., are read by the worship leaders *and the entire congregation.* When as a worshiper you are caught up in the emotion of the mob scene before Pilate, having to shout, "Give us Barrabas!" and "Crucify him!" it sends chills up your spine.

Some churches have used action-parables. To illustrate the morning theme, "I am the vine," from John's gospel, worshipers may be led to create lines or "branches" down the aisles, holding hands to symbolize their unity in Christ. An experience of segregation in worship might be employed to demonstrate the effects of prejudice, particularly if the "minority group" in the sanctuary had to serve the "majority" in some way, such as dusting their shoes without making eye contact. Well, you say, that's a kind of "simulation game," more appropriate for a workshop than worship—but some churches have recorded successful experiences of this type, and through this kind of informal drama the Word is proclaimed.

Mary Anne Burkholder of Geneva, Ohio, describes a kind of action-parable used for the children's sermon: "Periodically we improvise a Bible story. For example, 'The Man Sick with the Palsy.' With the help of a small rug, youngsters carried a child up the chancel steps to lift him through the "roof" to where he could be healed by Jesus." Children enjoy improvising, and they learn the story by enacting it! (Why not adults as well?)

Of course, the congregation doesn't have to be *physically* involved to be involved. Once I planned a "dialogue sermon" with a friend who interrupted me from his pew, then joined me on the platform to continue the dialogue. That surprised some worshipers; indeed, one elderly gentleman was heard to mutter, "Throw the bum out!" The two of us argued the paradox of priest and prophet, the extent to which we Christians are called to apparently contradictory roles, both comforting the afflicted and afflicting the comfortable. People were listening, at least—and it was for many a thoughtful and challenging service.

In summary, we can use these three criteria to measure the extent to which worship is *dramatic*: (1) there is congregational involvement, emotional if not physical; (2) there is crisis and conflict; (3) the worship re-enacts an important spiritual experience or rehearses that which is to be performed in the world.

So worship is inherently dramatic to the extent it possesses those elements. But there are special dramatic forms and methods that lend themselves to worship and often enhance it. To those forms we turn now. We shall first consider the sermon, then the use of dramatic "inserts," and finally, the kind of drama that may envelop and structure the entire liturgy.

The Sermon Spot

Many preachers, we say, have a dramatic "gift." They use rich imagery, convey excitement, tell stories creatively, develop conflict, and confront people compellingly. Some go beyond the usual preaching style to *impersonation*: the first-person sermon, in which the minister assumes the role of Peter, John, Zacchaeus, Mary Magdalene, the dove merchant in the temple, or the peanut-vendor at Golgotha. Well-researched monologues can have a significant impact, and they don't have to be delivered by the clergy: It may be advisable to assign one to someone with more acting experience or training.

Dialogues and trialogues make effective sermons too. Dialogue preaching was becoming popular during the sixties and seems to have peaked; but there are some still using it.[3] Such a dialogue may involve people with opposing viewpoints, as I've illustrated, or it may require impersonating biblical or historical figures. The congregation may be warned in advance or the dialogue may come as a surprise. My spiritual life was challenged when as a college student working at a Baptist retreat center, I experienced a service where someone interrupted a worship leader at the start of the Lord's Prayer! He argued that it should not be prayed: The worshipers were insincere or hypocritical because in life they took their "daily bread for granted," didn't really "forgive the debts" of others, etc. The interrupter spoke for the world's poor and dispossessed.

Also, we can use readers' theatre or straight drama in place of the standard sermon. This means that usually a script of about twenty to twenty-five minutes would work best in a Protestant context; of course, it must have the good artistic and theological qualities we're seeking. One example: I have used Norman Dietz' three-voice narrative, "Old Ymir's Clay Pot,"[4] on two or three occasions as a sermon-parable. It's an evocative retelling of the Christ-event in terms of Jeremiah's imagery of the pottery. And several churches have used my six-character play, *The Waiting Room*, as a dramatic sermon.

What about using radio and television scripts? A Presbyterian friend in Baltimore writes, "Going back as far as 1971, we used scripts obtained from the National Broadcasting Company, prepared by the Jewish Theological Seminary, New York City, for their radio series, "The Eternal Light." These were fifteen minute programs from the Old Testament—very suitable for chancel drama in place of a sermon."

Jack Kurtz' *A Matter of Death and Life*, and Robert Clausen's *The Gift and the Glory* each run twenty to thirty minutes, and would be excellent as dramatic sermons, as would certain of the chancel dramas of W. A. Poovey, Earl Reimer, Charles Williams, and others. Philip Turner's *Christ in the Concrete City* and *Watch at the World's End* are particularly good for liturgical use because of their rich poetic qualities and theological depth, but they are somewhat longer than a typical sermon.

Examples abound, especially from churches doing Youth Sunday services. But don't leave it up to the youth to fill the sermon-spot once a year. There are many creative methods of proclamation.

Dramatic Inserts

"As the prelude ended, an old, obviously poor woman wrapped in a shawl and wearing tennis shoes entered the sanctuary carrying a lantern. The lantern's flame was barely burning. She slowly proceeded to the rostrum and sat down, placing the lantern beside her. At this point Christmas carolers could be heard and a group of the singers entering, singing "Joy to the World." They formed a circle around the old lady as they sang. After a few moments they left the sanctuary, and the voices faded away. As the attention was directed back to the old woman, it was obvious that the lantern's flame was now burning at full strength. As she was leaving the sanctuary there was

91

intense silence. It was an electric moment. The silence finally was broken as I spoke John 1:4, 5 and 9."[5]

This is a description by Dr. Ray N. Howell of the Roxborough Baptist Church in North Carolina of a dramatic call to worship, one of several they used during Advent in 1983. Unlike dramatic sermons, which are longer and take more preparation time, dramatic vignettes are relatively easy to prepare and present. Drama can be used as the call to worship, invocation, call to confession, moment of absolution, introduction for the offering, children's spot, or to launch the sermon, capsulate its theme at the close, or provide a benediction!

There is precedent, as we have seen in Chapter Three. Dramatic inserts called *tropes* introduced the theatre revival in the liturgy of medieval churches. Specifically, it was the insertion of the *Quem Queritas* trope, followed by other dialogues inserted into the Mass, that paved the way for the mystery, miracle, and morality plays of the Middle Ages.

These days the liturgical inserts are not always biblical in character. They are indeed varied: Dance, dramatic stingers, mime, and readers' theatre are often used. In the church where I worship we formed a drama in worship committee and made drama a regular practice for a time: In one church year about one-third of the Sunday services included one or more dramatic inserts. Dance is beyond the province of this book, and I am devoting a separate chapter to readers' theatre, because of its utility. The remaining two forms which are most useful as dramatic inserts are stingers and mime.

The *stinger* is a mini-drama. It develops quickly to climax, then finishes with a punchline or "sting." "Looking Out for Number One" is the title we gave to a stinger used to lead into confessional prayer. The scene: standing below the marquee, a theatre manager talks with a young person applying for a job as an usher in the theatre. After discussing the applicant's qualifications—and having been assured by the boy that he's a responsible person—the manager asks:

> MANAGER: Well, then let me ask you this. Suppose one night a fire breaks out in the theatre. The curtain's going up in flames—it's bedlam. What would you do?
> APPLICANT: Oh, you wouldn't have to worry about me, sir. I'd get out all right!

The manager—and the audience—do a double take. The point is made about the innate self-centeredness of human beings.

Or, in the same spot one Sunday we used a sketch adapted from a well-known comic strip. A girl is stopping people on the street, holding a clipboard, anxiously asking them to sign a document "that absolves me of all blame for anything that goes wrong in the world—floods, fires, earthquakes, pogroms, rapes, abortions, mass murder, war—oh, thank you, sir, thank you, ma'am." And after she gets several people to sign she looks at the clipboard, counting names:

> PETITIONER: 97, 98, 99, 100 signatures! (*Then she groans, and looks at the audience*) But somehow I still feel guilty!

Stingers may be used at almost any point in worship. But they must, of course, relate—to that part of worship or to the overall theme—to say nothing of relating to the audience!

Using Mime

Mime, or *pantomime*, which in earlier times was called "dumbshow," has an ancient history. Mime is an action performed without words; in effect, pure gesture. Professionals often make a distinction between mime (described as the more abstract, symbolic art), and pantomime (a simpler art, a kind of nonverbal storytelling). But the distinction is fuzzy, I think, and not useful here: We shall use the terms interchangeably.

The word *pantomime*, from the Greek, may be broken into its prefix (*pan*) and root (*mimus*). *Pan* means "all," "every," or "universal," as in Pan-Hellenic Games or Pan-American Olympics, which presumably would involve every nation in the hemisphere. *Mimus* refers to imitation or an imitator. Hence, pantomime: imitation of all, or mimic of everything.

Mime is a valuable tool for acting training, as we'll see, but it can carry a potent message in itself. Consider Marcel Marceau's famous sketch, "The Mask-maker": Marceau sits in front of a table on which, apparently, there are masks he has made (we don't actually *see* them, or do we?) He tries them on, changing his facial expression with each. Finally he tries on a mask that has a very broad smile to it. At first he is pleased with his image in the mirror, he prances about happily, and then—he can't get it off! He works and works at it, and underneath the smiling interior we can feel the frustration or agony of a man trying to remove something that holds him captive. What a profound parable!

"The Mask-maker" is "straight mime" in that that there is total silence, or only soft background music. Such a mime has the advantage that nothing distracts the audience from the scene before them. Everett Robertson describes several such pantomimes in *Extra Dimensions in Church Drama.*[6] One of them, "The Lifetime," calls for a symbolic sound effect, the ticking of a clock. Both straight mime and narrated mime are illustrated in Burbridge and Watt's *Time to Act* (See especially "The Widow's Mites" and "The Light of the World.")[7]

Pantomime with narration is another form. A narrator or perhaps a chorus of voices tells a story as it is mimed by others. An acting team could mime illustrations during the sermon, or as a Bible passage was read, or perhaps embody the theme of an anthem or solo as it is sung. A group might brainstorm ideas for miming the theme of the worship service for several successive Sundays—those mimes might be given at the close of each service, to "sum it up."

Also, there is pantomimed action with a punchline. The sketch is completely silent until the end, then the audience is surprised with a line coming out of the blue! Would it jog the mind, for example, if a new twist were given to the parable of the prodigal son? Suppose at the end of the mime the father says to the prodigal, "This is the third fatted calf I've prepared for you, son. When *are* you going to settle down?"

Or, consider a mime-with-punchline I developed with the help of a senior high group: We enacted the story of Genesis 2, with God snapping his fingers and Adam and Eve rising out of the group. The snake sidles up and points out a tree (being mimed, of course) with an imaginary apple hanging from a branch. Adam takes the apple from Eve, reluctantly, then eats it with relish and throws away the core; to which the tree responds, "Litterbug!" (Would this launch a sermon on stewardship of the earth?)

Finally, consider the monologue-and-mime combination. . . . A college drama team developed a sketch called "The Party." A young woman's sitting at an invisible desk in her bedroom, working on homework one evening and taking phone calls from friends. Behind her is a male actor, an embodied Christ. Over the phone she tells a friend that she's a disciple of Christ now—her life has been transformed. The friend wants her to go to a party that evening, "a bed and drug scene," and she declines.

94

Then comes another phone call, and she's surprised and elated to find that it's "Mike," someone she really wants to date—but he wants to take her to that same party! She struggles with her feelings, finally agrees to go with Mike to the party, jumps up and primps in front of a mirror, then mimes opening the door and calling to her mother, "Mom, I'm tired, I'm going to bed early tonight." She turns and almost runs into the Christ-figure, still shadowing her. She stops, looks him full in the face, and then spins around him to the window, which she attempts to open to make her escape. He follows her; and she turns twice to urge him to leave: "You can't follow me! You won't like it there! You won't fit in!" He persists, so finally, exasperated and angry, she spins away from the window screaming at him; and she slaps his hands, nailing him, in effect, on the lines, "I don't want you there! You don't own me!" There is a long pause: Realizing what she has said and done, she bows her head, facing the audience. The Christ-figure stands next to her with his back to the audience, arms outstretched . . . a moving image indeed.

Pantomime is a serious art, deserving of more space than we can give it here; and the training for a professional is extensive. Here are just a few words of advice for nonprofessionals beginning to work with mime:

(1) Use the whole body to express yourself—there is more to you than just the face and hands!

(2) Be aware of invisible objects on stage. Concentrate. Don't forget to open a closed door and close it behind you, instead of walking through it! And if you pick up a glass of water and drink from it, don't just drop it— put it down again. (I have seen an actor carry a baby on stage, and then just drop it!)

(3) When you're holding an invisible object, be sure to leave space between your fingers. To get the knack, actually pick up and hold real objects first, then mime the actions. Sense the texture and weight of an object, and be sure you can feel the weight when you're lifting an imaginary suitcase or throwing an invisible spear. If you can't feel it, they won't see it!

(4) Keep physical properties to a minimum. Usually mime is performed on a bare stage, but you may want a chair or one or two objects that are important to the scene. If the scene has to be introduced or titled, you can put the title on a sign and hold it up, or place it on an easel.

(5) Be precise, be clear, and try to finish every action that you begin.

(6) Believe in your audience. Force them to visualize. They have imaginations—work with them!

To review: Mime and stingers, as well as speech choirs and readers' theatre, have the ability to enhance worship.

The Dramatic Structuring of Worship

Now consider some ways in which drama may envelop worship, structuring the liturgy as a whole.

One approach is through *clowning*. At the top of the chapter I mentioned an experience when clowning provided the structure for worship. Although some people can't relate to clowns (and I think it has something to do with being "threatened" by clowns as a child), Christian clowning is becoming more popular: The *Church Drama Newsletter* (Southern Baptist) contains a "Clown Corner" as a regular feature, in which church clown ministries are highlighted along with workshops and conferences for Christian clowns. Clown ministry groups often perform at children's hospitals, retirement centers, and other events; and some offer liturgical experiences in their own churches or for other congregations.

The traditional *pageant* provides another structured worship event. A pageant is a rather spectacular blend of narrative scripture, choral recitation, song (sometimes), and acting. Pageants are traditionally performed at the holy seasons, especially Advent. Pageants are generally celebrative, and although many lack artistic depth, they provide an uplifting communal event for the congregation to rally around.

The liturgical dramas of Olov Hartman, a Swedish playwright, are perhaps a step beyond the traditional church pageant. Hartman has developed some elaborate, colorful dramas based on scripture and using a powerful free verse that often approximates the rhythm and function of the ancient Greek chorus. Mr. Hartman has arranged passages from both Testaments imaginatively in such plays as *The Fiery Furnace*,[8] juxtaposing materials that may not seem at first to go together; the connections may be obscure and some of the dialogue is stiff, but on the whole the result is a moving dramatic development of a biblical theme.

Pageants do come in many forms. I was privileged to witness a unique Advent event in 1984 in Syracuse, New York, when Open Hand Theatre presented a "puppetry pageant" titled, "As Starlight Grows the Winter Rose." The troupe used a church sanctuary where the pews had been removed to provide adequate space for the huge 15-25 foot puppets and ranging dramatic action. Created by Geoffrey Navias, who had worked with Bread and Puppet Theatre, the huge puppet figures, manipulated by troupe members, were central—but the action included ordinary mime as well as music and dance, actors on stilts, and signs floated from the balconies. Over eighty people helped create and produce the show, whose scenario followed the Advent accounts in Matthew and Luke, freely interpreted and with a subtle political emphasis.

Consider the Annunciation scene. Mary stood in front of a fabric backdrop—a painted landscape with slits through which properties could be handed actors—it seemed "alive" at times. Above her, two huge puppet faces protruded from the upper balconies left and right, identical angels overlooking the action. As a trumpet fanfare opened the scene, Mary stood on the floor, bewildered by two huge cardboard hands that were slid down wires from the balcony, pointing at her imperiously as if to say, "You are the One!" These were followed with a huge sign strung across a wire overhead: "Fear Not." Singing was heard, during which someone wrapped Mary in a large banner bearing the words, "Blessed Are You," and an angel on stilts danced about the forestage. Other scenes were equally creative and stimulating. My sense of wonder was restoked by this unusual perspective on Advent, and the drama helped me to find connections between that ancient event and the world in which I live.

Finally—still thinking about ways in which biblically-based drama can structure worship—consider some innovations introduced at the 8:30 Sunday morning experimental worship of Hope Reformed Church in Holland, Michigan. Dr. George Ralph writes that a task force of creative pastors and laypersons has created some unique liturgical experiences over the years: "A particular interest of mine is deriving liturgical structure (rather than simply content) from biblical sources. Several years ago I based a major portion of a service on the Genesis accounts of creation, fall, Cain and Abel—with one bit of business suggested by performances I had seen of Jean-Claude van Italle's *The Serpent*. A bit later I tried an entire service following the progression of the Book of Job."[9]

Professor Ralph reports that both worked well and produced a positive response from worshipers. I found his Genesis service so creative and unique that I secured his permission to reprint it

97

in our resource section. "Darkness and Hope" is a creative example of using scriptural material to structure worship and to provide a meaningful frame in which to examine ourselves and our lifestyles as children of God in the world.

To Conclude . . .

In Chapter Five we have examined the inherent dramatic qualities in the liturgy. We have also examined ways and means of inserting relevant dramatic material—stingers and mime, in particular, that will enhance or embody the worship themes. Finally, we discussed drama that encompasses worship, creating its own liturgy, imposing its own order on the event.

Remember that worship, besides its other functions, enables us to *rehearse* our faith-attitudes and our work as God's change-agents in the world. Inside and outside the sanctuary walls we are the players and God the audience, before whom our discipleship is embodied and enacted.

6

Readers' Theatre

Readers' theatre is a relatively simple, inexpensive method of adapting and staging dramatic material. Take an evocative, exciting piece of literature—anything from Daniel 3 or one of the gospel stories to Aesop or a satire by Art Buchwald or Arthur Hoppe—prepare lively scripts with parts for several voices, position them on a bare platform, the chancel steps, or one end of the fellowship hall, and if they have been thoroughly rehearsed to read the material freely and expressively, the audience will not mind the fact that they are holding books. Indeed, you may have some powerful theatre!

Unlike conventional theatre, there is little or no scenery and costuming, and often no special lighting. In conventional theatre we pretend that a scene is physically happening on stage before an audience; in readers' theatre we convey an imaginary scene to the auditors' minds. Readers' theatre is *theatre of the mind*: It demands a fuller use of the imagination than even conventional theatre requires. But readers' theatre, with its simplicity and ease of staging, often provides the answer in situations where time and limited resources preclude a full-scale dramatic production.

Finding Suitable Materials

We are not limited to plays in using the readers' theatre approach. It permits us to dramatize any literature that has certain special qualities: evocative language, interesting characters, absorbing or suspenseful action. (But of course there must be a completeness to it—you can cull a scene from a longer work, like a biography or a novel, but it must be satisfying in itself.)

In *Readers Theatre Comes to Church*, reprinted recently by Meriwether,[1] I have included many sample scripts showing the diversity of readers' theatre materials. Often humorous or provocative essays or newspaper columns may be adapted and performed; short stories such as Silverstein's *The Giving Tree* or Jones' "Lying Offshore" from *To the Crowds in Parables* make exciting readers' theatre; absorbing novels like St. Johns' *Tell No Man* or fantasies like C. S. Lewis' *The Great Divorce* are possible; biographies and autobiographies, if they contain colorful anecdotes and conversations, are likely; and certain poetry, generally the epic or narrative type, may be possible. But the most likely and abundant source of scripts for readers' theatre is the short story.

In my book on readers' theatre, as well as in the excellent *Readers Theatre Handbook* by Coger and White,[2] detailed steps for adapting a script from its original material are given. This is not the place for such detail, but as an illustration I am including a brief parable by Wes Seelinger, originally printed in *Faith at Work* (1972) and used here by permission of the author. In adapting the piece I restyled the narrative for three voices and added frog sounds to strengthen the whimsical effect. Notice that VOICE 1 carries the narration, VOICES 2 and 3 provide character lines and sound effects:

Froghood

by Wes Seelinger

VOICE 1: Ever feel like a frog?

VOICES 2 & 3: Ribbit, ribbit, ribbit, ribbit, ribbit!

VOICE 1: Frogs feel tired, listless, lethargic, lazy, and ugly. They know they're not handsome or beautiful, and they pity themselves. They have no place to go and nothing to do, and their entire existence is confined to the small green lily pad on which they sit thinking and idly watching the tadpoles swim by. In that respect, frogs are a lot like people. I know, because a frog told me.

VOICE 2: I feel sad,

VOICE 3: mad,

VOICE 2: lazy,

VOICE 3: ugly,

VOICE 2: drooped,

VOICE 3: pooped.

VOICES 2 & 3: I feel like I'm just sitting here and life's passed me by. Ribbit, ribbit, ribbit, ribbit, ribbit!

VOICE 1: But this story has a happy ending. That frog I met just wasn't what he appeared to be.

VOICE 2: I'm not really a frog

VOICE 3: but a beautiful princess

VOICES 2 & 3: disguised as a frog!

VOICE 1: Long ago the princess had been zapped by a wicked witch because of some imagined wrong done by the princess' parents. But as you know, there is always an antidote for a witch's spell. In this case the remedy was a handsome prince. He happened to be out walking his dog one day when he came upon the pond in which our frog was sitting upon her lily pad. The prince had the power to see beyond appearances, and he could tell that the frog was not what it appeared to be. Throwing caution to the winds, the prince stepped into the pond and planted a fat kiss right on that big green frog. (With appropriate gestures:)

VOICE 2: ZAP!

VOICE 3: BANG!

VOICES 2 & 3: SWOOSH!

VOICE 1: And the big green frog turned back into the beautiful princess. They were married and lived happily ever after . . . except, of course, for the usual domestic discord. So . . . what is the task of the church? To kiss frogs, of course.

VOICES 2 & 3: Oooh? Oooooh! (With optional "ribbits" to end the scene)

"Froghood" lends itself to "hamming": broad mime, business, special vocal effects. The readers should *sound* "sad, mad, lazy, ugly, dropped, pooped," etc. They can do a shoulder-motion on the "ribbits" to simulate frog movement. They can play to each other on the mid-section, "I'm not really a frog but a beautiful princess disguised as a frog!" and hug each other in their joy! And if they are opposite sex they could even kiss each other—or throw wet, noisy kisses—on "ZAP! BANG! SWOOSH!" The vocal inflections and facial expressions need to be just right, of course, on the "Oooh? Oooooh!" at the end. The first is a slow, surprised question, the second a very definite, "I get it!" reaction. Note: Readers' theatre isn't a passive medium—a lot of feeling can be conveyed nonverbally, through posture, gesture, and body tension.

In the church where I've held membership for almost twenty years, we have done much more readers' theatre than conventional drama. This is because we have had some talented readers available, and because most of us are too busy—or think we are too busy—to memorize lines in a play. But we have rehearsed carefully and I believe that 90 percent of our presentations have been effective.

Very few religious materials have been written *especially for* readers' theatre. The sixteen parables in my *Happy Tales, Fables, and Plays* would be an exception, as would Jack Kurtz' *Gargoyles, Plastic Balls, and Soup*. W. H. Auden's unique Christmas "oratorio for voices," *For the Time Being*, becomes effective as readers' theatre *if* you have a sophisticated, literate congregation and extremely skillful interpreters. During Advent it can be a growth experience for the cast as they struggle with its profound ideas and abstruse images, but it may be difficult to communicate to an audience.

At our church we have adapted various kinds of materials for reading in worship. These would include parts of plays (e.g., scenes from Mueller's *Eyes Upon the Cross*, Wilder's *Our Town*, Bolt's *A Man for All Seasons*, Ibsen's *An Enemy of the People*), short stories like Daniel 3 and Jones' "Lying Offshore," humorous essays like Martinez' "Where Have All the Flowers Gone?" and scenes from religious novels (e.g. Douglas' *The Robe*, St. Johns' *Tell No Man*).

In addition—largely because I was often unable to find material written on a specific theme that we could adapt for worship—I have written a good many short readers' theatre scripts. No doubt you have some creative people in your congregation—perhaps even professional writers—who could produce some meaningful short scripts. Oscar Rumpf has written some fine modern choric readings (*Cries from the Hurting Edges of the World*)[3] that border on readers' theatre and illustrate how contemporary material (commercials, political slogans, etc.) can be welded into an engaging, provocative script. Very timely material can be developed from reading today's newspaper—note what Arthur Hoppe and Art Buchwald do in the topical, satiric vein. Original material can be written to awaken Christian concern about such issues as pollution, war, poverty, imperialism, drugs, sexual standards, and the price of bananas! The task isn't easy; perhaps it's as difficult as writing a new play, but it's fun for the creative mind.

The rest of us, who haven't the time or talent to write original stories or poetry, will have to adapt material written by others. If you don't want to do that, look for material that's already been adapted. There is a growing body of readers' theatre adaptations, some of it with spiritual themes and subjects. One good source of such material is Contemporary Drama Service, which has published several packets of readers' theatre scripts, performance-ready, by Melvin R. White, myself, and others.

Staging Readers' Theatre

The twin keys to readers' theatre are *simplicity* and *suggestion*. If the aim is to stimulate the listeners' imaginations the staging may be kept simple yet suggestive. This will be good news to many people, who prefer to avoid the expense and hassle of constructing scenery, stitching costumes, and otherwise getting several church committees all hot and bothered about a production which never comes off quite as well as it should technically.

But staging *is* important. Briefly, we need to consider the type of eye focus being used, positioning and spacing, making entrances and exits, and the use of special effects.

Locus refers to the place of an action; *focus* to the placement of gaze, or the actor-interpreter's eye contact. In the typical stage-play the locus and the eye contact is onstage: Actors look at each other when they talk to one another. In readers' theatre, however, *offstage focus* is often used: When they look up from their scripts—which should be often—readers will gaze out over the heads of the audience rather than at another reader. And when the story calls for some gesture—a bow, a salute, the use of a tool or gun—the reader should mime the gesture *toward the mirror-image* rather than to the onstage reader. This makes for an interesting visual effect.

Purists prefer offstage focus because it tends to throw the scene into the audience, project it in the midst of them. In rehearsal, the trick is to direct your readers to pick a spot on the back wall as if they were seeing themselves in a mirror; that is, one would speak to another character in the story as if that character were opposite to its reader, projected to the back wall. This diagram will show how the focus of several readers will converge at some point above the audience and about halfway to the back wall:

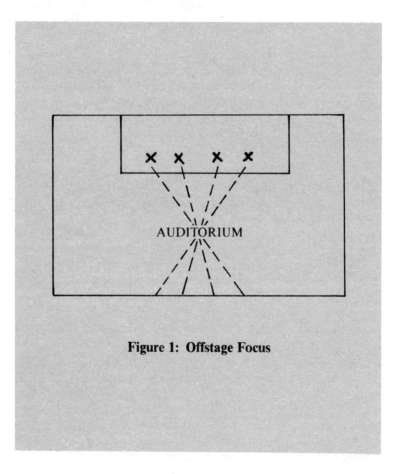

Figure 1: Offstage Focus

There are times and places, however, when "normal" *onstage focus* will be used; and if your cast rebels against offstage focus because it "feels wrong" to them, it may have to be used. Also, it is helpful sometimes, although a performance may be generally offstage, to switch to onstage focus for a climactic scene—just to give it more strength. (This is not to say that an offstage focus scene will be weak, only that a sudden change will highlight its importance.) But you need to avoid inconsistent focus for it will be confusing to the audience.

The third type of focus, or gaze, is *narrative focus*. Readers using onstage or offstage focus will not be looking directly at the members of the audience; but a narrator will be. He or she will be making eye contact with individuals in the audience. It goes without saying that any narrator must be articulate and personable, and able to carry the storyline with verve and pace.

It should also go without saying that your readers know their material well, and have rehearsed it enough to get their eyes, for the most part, off the printed page. But it must be said; and it is something you have to work at in rehearsal: "Get your eyes up! Get your nose out of the book! Come on, now, pick up that phrase and give it to me—out here!" Poor readers cannot do this, but average readers can generally be trained to do a passable job of focus—and it must be done, despite the risk of a reader occasionally losing his or her place.

Incidentally, some college productions involve total memorization—books are not carried. This is sometimes called "Chamber Theatre," especially with prose fiction. Stage blocking is similar to that used in conventional theatre, and the interpreter-actors have more freedom of movement; but again, there is no attempt at realistic staging, and the narrator-storyteller is extremely important.

Next, *positioning and spacing.* Traditionally, stools and lecterns are the basic properties in readers' theatre. The advantage of a stool is that it is portable and readers can turn easily while sitting; groups doing lots of readers' theatre may want to buy stools in several sizes. But chairs, platforms, boxes, etc., may also be used for sitting, and in many productions you may want all your readers standing.

The lectern offers the possibility of doing more gesture and body action, since the script may be placed on it, freeing the arms, but at the same time it hides the body somewhat. My own preference is to dispense with lecterns and have my readers hold the script in one hand, gesturing with the other. The script may also be used as a "property" in the imaginary scene—a reader may offer it to another to suggest the giving of a gift, or hold it over the head to suggest a hat, an umbrella, a placard, or weight-lifting!

Keep in mind that readers do not have to be static—they may or may not remain sitting or standing in the same location throughout the performance. This will depend largely on how long and how complicated the material is. We try to avoid unnecessary movement, which in brief scenes seems especially awkward. It may be helpful to plan some limited or symbolic movements, however; and often the narrator has more freedom of movement since he or she is omniscient, perhaps, or is "offering" the whole scene to the audience and takes a custodial relationship to the cast.

Take a simple three-reader story like Seelinger's "Froghood," and consider the possible ways readers may be positioned. If you have steps or levels the readers may be given a vertical arrangement: They may sit or stand with their faces appearing one above the other. This is like watching a baseball game from behind home plate—you keep pitcher, catcher, batter, and umpire within your narrow view. The vertical pattern is fine for some pieces, such as Norman Dietz' thoughtful fable, "Old Ymir's Clay Pot," from his *Fables and Vaudevilles and Plays*, but perhaps not for "Froghood." Here two of the readers (with the frog voices) are paired and need to be together, I think, and probably somewhat separated from READER 1. So I would use a simple triangle, with READER 1 standing slightly downstage of READERS 2 & 3, or the reverse. Other methods you could try: Put READER 1 on a platform upstage and to the right or left of READERS 2 & 3; put READER 1 on a bench or stool, with 2 & 3 standing behind; or put 2 & 3 on the bench, with 1 standing behind. You might need to bring them off their duffs later, at least for the "ZAP! BANG! SWOOSH!" at the end. Note the possibilities in Figure 2.

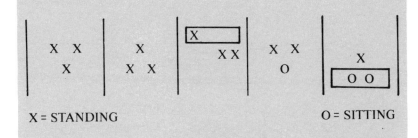

X = STANDING   O = SITTING

Figure 2: Five Ways of Staging "Froghood," A 3-Person Reading

Three-person readings, of course, are easy to stage compared to something like the Book of Job or the novel, *Tell No Man*. The material needs to be examined carefully to divide it into scenes and episodes, with staging for each according to the prominence and relationships among the characters. With large-cast readers' theatre productions you will find it helpful to have several stage levels. A chancel with steps is fine for most readers' theatre, and if you're in the social hall of the church, maybe some low platforms, boxes, or risers will help.

In staging an adaptation of C. S. Lewis' *The Great Divorce* as readers' theatre for a college chapel, I felt that the key figures were the narrator (Lewis, the storyteller) and George MacDonald (his spiritual mentor) so I elevated these readers upstage. Then I staggered six chairs left and right to accommodate the other interpreters, with each reading more than one character. The story is largely a series of conversations between pairs of characters, the "Ghosts" of earth and "Spirits" from heaven; to help the audience understand, I put a bench down center and had the pairs of readers move to that bench for their particular dialogues at the right time. Offstage focus was used. When a conversation was finished, the two interpreters returned to their original seats. (See Figure 3, below.)

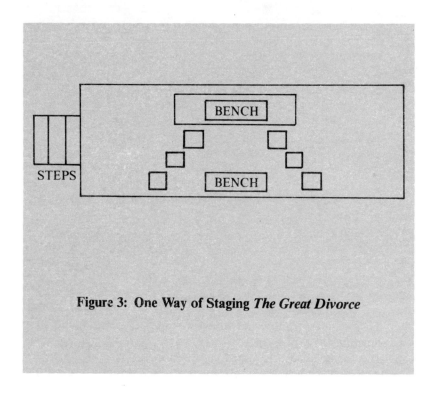

Figure 3: One Way of Staging *The Great Divorce*

You are not likely to stage readers' theatre in the round, because of the nature of locus and focus in readers' theatre. But sometimes you can position readers facing each other across a circle, or even across space held by the audience. This would work when your readers were divided into groups, arguing or contending for something. The result would be to place the audience physically—as well as psychologically—in the middle. When the dynamic or tone of the story changed, however, your readers would move to another position.

Entrances and exits. How do you get your readers into and out of a scene? This is important, for even in a short story there may be characters who enter and leave the action and it's wise to do something visual with entrances and exits—don't just have readers standing around trying to look invisible!

In conventional theatre, we have characters enter through stage doors or from the wings, physically walking onto stage space or out of it. But with readers' theatre, a theatre of the imagination, we don't want to be literal. To have readers enter the action, you can have them (a) stand, if sitting (b) sit, if standing (c) raise their heads (d) open their books (e) turn their faces to the audience, or (f) more than one of the above. The reverse would be true for readers who are leaving a scene; that is, if your system involves raising/lowering the head, they would lower it when leaving.

Probably the most common method of leaving a scene is turning one's back to the audience, and then facing the audience when entering. Like other conventions, the audience will understand and accept it if it is used consistently.

As to costuming: Again, simple is fine. But clearly, your readers' apparel must at least be non-distracting. Often you want a uniform appearance with readers dressed in black and white, or in white shirts, or all with gray vests, or whatever. You may want to add some special touches, particularly when your readers double in parts. Giving different characters identifying hats, for example—as farmers, sailors, gentlemen, etc.—may enhance the performance. And if there are two or more different factions in the narrative—Union and Confederate soldiers for example—you may want to at least use contrasting colors in dress. But we seldom use "period" costume in readers theatre.

Finally, *special effects*. Staging readers' theatre is relatively simple, but occasionally some special effects may enhance a production. Lighting is normally just turned on and off, and some argue that the entire house should be lit during the performance, not just the stage, which reduces the aesthetic distance between the artists and the audience. But in some cases spotlighting or mood lighting will be useful, and sometimes slide projections add interest.

In doing a college readers' theatre production of a short spoof of Gothic tales, *The Thirteenth Skull*, by Franklyn Styne, I had my readers sitting on stools in a semicircle. Above each was a red lightbulb, and when each of them "entered" he or she reached up and yanked the cord to turn it on. With blue-red backlighting the effect was properly spooky, and the readers had barely enough light to read! For another show, St. Exupery's *The Little Prince*, we projected illustrative drawings on a screen at center stage, with readers positioned stage right and left. And we used double imagery for a scene taken from St. Johns' moving novel, *Tell No Man*. The climax comes when a young girl, Deedee, who has just died in an automobile accident, is carried by her boyfriend into the living room of the parsonage, and the pastor and his wife and the girl's parents rush toward them. We showed the boy carrying the girl's body in shadows thrown from backstage on the scrim backdrop; at the same time the Retzlaffs and the Gavins moved toward the audience as if Deedee were being laid on the apron of the stage. The double image was intriguing and underscored the intensity of the moment.

Audio effects may help at times. We added some drumming to help strengthen the climax during the reading of the martyrdom of Sir Thomas More in a scene from *A Man for All Seasons*. Excerpts from Saint-Saens' *Carnival of the Animals* are suggested for use with a reading of George Orwell's *Animal Farm*, by its adapter, Nelson Bond. And Dylan Thomas' *Under Milk Wood*, a warm, sensuous, poetic description of a day in the life of a Welsh village, calls for a number of mood sounds. In our college production they were all vocalized by readers—chickens, cows, dogs barking, church bells, etc. In a professional show that I attended they used a sound track instead. I prefer the use of actors' voices.

Now . . . having said all of this about staging and effects, there really are no rules in readers' theatre! There are methods and techniques—and we have stressed consistency within a production—but there are no ironclad rules. Be creative!

Composite Programs

Do you like to read widely? Do you file or keep references for what you read? You might like to prepare a *composite* readers' theatre program. Such a program would include several different pieces of literature arranged on a given theme: war and peace, love and marriage, politics, integrity, faith, missions, etc; or, perhaps a program arranged for Advent, for Lent, or for another holiday or special occasion, sacred or secular. Here is a composite program for Advent developed by Dr. Melvin R. White, formerly of California State College, Hayward:

Christmas Comes But Once A Year

The Past . . .
> St. Luke 2:1-20
> "The Shepherd Who Would Not Go," by Heywood Broun
> Massachusetts Statute, 1660

The Present . . .
> "The Second Shepherd," by Albert Howard Carter
> "Christmas Card Quandary," from "Merry Christmas Plus Peace on Earth," by Art Buchwald
> "The Founding of a Business Miracle," and "A Christmas Story," by Russell Baker
> "How Mrs. Santa Claus Saved Christmas," by Phyllis McGinley
> "The Errors of Santa Claus," by Stephen Leacock
> "The Twelve Mistakes of Christmas, Not Including that Partridge in the Pear Tree," by Ogden Nash

And . . .
> Exerpts from "The Hope of the World," by Robert Quillen

Professor Todd Lewis of Biola University, who has practically made a career of developing fine composite scripts, writes:

> I think that the compiled script is the answer to several nagging questions for anyone interested in doing readers' theatre in religious situations. First, a compiled script makes use of all kinds of literature—short and long prose pieces, monologues, play scenes, poems, letters, prayers, scripture—and allows the compiler/director to formulate these smaller elements into a tailor-made script for the audience and the time. Second, I believe that readers' theatre should combine these three elements: Acting, Literature, and Rhetoric. By using various forms of literature, you can compile a script of your own and make a "persuasive/rhetorical statement," using the literature to share your perspectives.[4]

Professor Lewis begins with a single piece that he particularly appreciates, then adds additional material that seems to "go with it." He collects the material in a folder until there is more than he can possibly use; then he re-reads the material to see whether any meaningful sequence comes to mind. There is a brooding period, which takes anywhere from one week to two months. "But it's quite valuable," he writes, "because the compiler/director needs to understand what he or she would like to say so that the traditional material (which is the work of the compiler) will further the theme.... Sometimes a recurring phrase or slogan will help carry the theme through. I always try to tie the previous piece in with the next piece by referring to content in both as you move from one to another."

Professor Lewis keeps a file of "possibles" for future use, gleaned from his readings. He finds that particular periodicals provide excellent materials for dramatizing, such as *Campus Life, Wittenburg Door* (for satirical stuff), and *His Magazine*. Also, he incorporates material from Christian books and plays as well as original monologues and dialogues. "The biggest problem," he says, "is that it takes time to find just the right combination of literature."

Finally ...

Readers' theatre has some distinct advantages: it doesn't require a complete memorization, it can be staged simply and is therefore less expensive, and it can be used to dramatize various kinds of literature apart from plays.

But don't let these patent benefits deceive you into doing readers' theatre as a quick fix, a shortcut that leaves everyone unhappy with the finished product. Conventional theatre is a better option than readers' theatre when you're working with unread people—today's generation of TV watchers who never learned to read or enjoy reading, or never read good literature. For such, the readers' theatre script is an albatross. Remember that poorly read readers' theatre is worse than doing none at all!

For readers' theatre you have to find people who enjoy reading and have some talent for it—there are still many such people around! Handpick your readers carefully.

Also, we need to weigh the problem from the auditors' side. Most of our listeners are conditioned by hours of movie and television-watching to expect all the scenery to be there. When they discover that they have to really work at the task of listening *with imagination*, they may tune out—unless the readers are capable and the material is lively. I suppose this is why readers' theatre scripts, in general, tend to be shorter than most stageplays—to better hold listeners' attention.

On the practical side, you need to consider the abilities and skills of your potential performers, and what they're used to doing; also, the deadline your group faces. If time is short you may lean toward doing readers' theatre instead of memorized drama, but never give your readers the impression that readers' theatre can be whipped up overnight! Even a fifteen minute presentation will require several rehearsals, unless your readers are very gifted indeed.

Still, readers' theatre is fun! Adapting material is fun, and so is the performance of it. And if the material has depth and the performance is vital and vibrant, it will engage the audience, stretching imaginations and fostering faith.

Readers' theatre may be quite right for the church or campus dramatist who lacks time, resources, or the personnel required to mount a full-scale, conventional production.

7

Church Productions: Doing and Making-Do

One of the early newspapers in the Ozarks contained this revue of a public "entertainment": "It was soothing, stirring, and satisfying. It was so soothing that part of the audience went to sleep. It was so stirring that part of the audience went home. It was so satisfying that those who stayed to see the performance never wanted to see it again."

The unwritten rule is, "Thou shalt not produce dull plays!" Effective play production involves selecting quality material, developing capable actors, and presenting it well. But some will say, "We're so limited in what we do. We have no stage in our church, and the chancel's much too small for plays!"

Nonsense. There are no chancels too small for dramatic events. A divided chancel with pulpit and lectern on either side allows for dialogue sermons, at least, and if there are chancel steps or levels some interesting readers theatre, mime, and simple plays are possible. Readers theatre can be presented anywhere, as long as there is room for two or more people to stand. And if the pulpit furniture can be removed, there is often more room in the chancel than people realize.

114

There is always stage space. Wherever you place your per-formers, that's your stage—the lounge, the fellowship hall, the front steps of the church, the parking lot. A large church I know has made a fine stage at one end of their gymnasium by creatively arranging risers and platforms; smaller churches without gyms often use an area within the fellowship hall—either at one end or in the middle of the hall—as an acting area; or by adding an extension platform to the chancel, provide additional perfor-mance space in the sanctuary.

Many churches have "real" stages, usually built into one end of the fellowship hall. Any stage with a picture-frame opening, usually with curtains that can be drawn across it, is called a *proscenium* stage. Unfortunately, many of these built-in church stages are small and cramped, without adequate wings or back-stage area, and they may lack proper lighting. Often the lighting has been placed directly overhead so that the actors have to stand well upstage to be lit; and sometimes there are footlights, which are considered today to be almost useless.

So, to be useful, the built-in church stage may need to be extended beyond the proscenium to give it more depth by adding a raised platform "apron" in front of the stage, or by using steps and a floor-level acting area. Of course, you will have to add lighting instruments to cover the additional area. All of this is to your advantage: If you can get your actors out beyond the proscenium into the lap of the audience you will get your audience more involved—and your actors will be heard more easily. More about lighting later.

We can assume that most colleges have an adequate stage with reasonably good lighting, and some professional expertise on call. This chapter is primarily aimed at those Christians work-ing in local churches with limited resources and largely untrained personnel. Although this is not a book of detailed production techniques, I intend to review enough of the important produc-tion questions in this chapter to provide help for relatively inex-perienced church dramatists. For additional detail, consult such worthy books as those by Carl Allensworth,[1] James Hull Miller,[2] and others.

We have looked at the use of drama in worship elsewhere. In this chapter I want us to primarily think about the special church production: a sizable one-act, or a longer play, presented as an event in itself.

The Production Team

Ideally, a production team in a large church or campus theatre department would involve the following persons:

1. the director, responsible for the production's artistic side—casting, rehearsals, the overall quality of the play . . .

2. the assistant director, who "subs" for the director when the latter must be absent, who often serves as prompter and "gopher" during rehearsals, and who may do the telephoning . . .

3. the stage manager, who has to get the stage ready for rehearsals and performances, who oversees the placement of properties and scenery . . .

4. the designer, who creates the idea for the set together with the director, and oversees the construction of scenery . . .

5. the technical director, who is responsible for the costuming, lighting, sound, and makeup of the production, but may delegate those tasks to others . . .

6. the producer, who is responsible for finding funds and controlling the budget, paying expenses, handling publicity and ticket sales . . .

7. and the house manager, who arranges for ushers, controls the seating, lighting, and heat in the auditorium before and during the performance, and who sells tickets at the door if that is done.

This is the *ideal*. In actual practice, even in large churches, these functions are seldom handled by seven different people; generally they are combined, and often combined into just two or three main roles, with additional duties delegated. These may be the roles of director and stage manager.

Unhappily, in small churches or on small college campuses, the overworked director may wind up shopping for props, calling newspapers, even running off the program on a mimeograph—unless he or she is good at involving people and delegating responsibility (but, as we all know, sometimes it's quicker to do it yourself!) Details, details!

Play Selection

You have to select a play before you can produce one. People complain of a dearth of good religious drama today, but there is a considerable amount if you know where to find it.

116

You need to decide initially what kind of a play you want. What is the occasion? Is it Advent? Easter? Thanksgiving? Pentecost? World Order Sunday? The dedication of a new sanctuary? There are plays that address a variety of special occasions and seasonal celebrations of faith.

Do you want a play that's complete in itself or one that begs discussion? There are many plays that resolve themselves, leaving little room for discussion, such as Goodman's old classic, *Dust of the Road*, or the popular Passion Play, *Christ in the Concrete City*; others leave you hanging, guessing, wondering, or doubting, like Eve McFalls's *The Case Against Eve* or Rutenborn's *The Sign of Jonah*, or Edna St. Vincent Millay's *Aria da Capo*. The latter tend to be more symbolic and abstract, so you need to ask whether your audience is prepared to concentrate. Will they be challenged by *Aria da Capo* or turned off by it? Also, a number of social problem plays, fantasies, and dramatic parables have been written for discussion—and many have discussion questions or "probes" attached.

Serious plays function mainly in three ways, to teach, arouse, or affirm. (Technically didactic, agitative, or celebratory.) You need to choose a play in relation to what you expect of it, what your purpose is related to your audience. The subject matter needs to be considered as well—do you want a biblical or quasi-biblical play, a historical play, or something in the morality play vein? The occasion needs to be considered. Also, the question of audience readiness: Is your audience ready for the kind of play you're presenting? Maybe it's too abstruse, too daring or too challenging for *this* audience at *this* time and place.

Finally, consider your own resources. How many people can you expect to show for auditions? How many capable actors can you count on, male or female? Can they handle difficult characters? Verse dialogue? Mime? Do you have a variety of ages available? Are there any special casting needs in the play that you're considering, e.g. for a small child or a British accent or a seven-foot basketball player? How theatrical is the play—does it require technical effects you cannot produce? Difficult scene changes? Projected scenery? Backlighting? Unusual period costuming?

Having answered such questions, you are ready to make your selection. You should have catalogs from the prominent play producers on hand. (See the list of sources in the Resource section.)

117

Forgive a final moralism: Don't be put off by plays that require the payment of royalties. These are often the best plays And by all means, pay the royalty! Some people earn their living by writing—even, believe it or not, playwrights—and you deprive them of their livelihood if you skip payment. (A laborer is worthy of his/her hire, according to scripture!) Enough said.

Auditions and Casting

Once a play is selected, dear reader—and let's assume that you're the director—*study it*. Identify its theme and consider how that theme's been developed through the episodes or scenes. Identify the climax and rhythm of the play, what the changing moods are, what drives the characters. Once you have these things in mind you can develop character descriptions to use in auditions and in rehearsing your actors. The auditions should be well-publicized, even though you may privately ask certain persons to try out because you appreciate their talent or experience.

Consider the following in selecting your cast. Innate talent is one factor, naturally, and how the auditioner seems physically to fit the role is another; but *dependability* and *coachability* are just as important. Nothing is more aggravating than actors who are absent or late to rehearsals—these people waste everyone's time. A person who is ten minutes late with six people waiting has wasted sixty minutes of others' time! (Make this point with your cast!) On one occasion we rejected a talented student actor auditioning for *Godspell* because in another production of the same play elsewhere his attitude had been a major morale problem for the cast.

Coachability has to do with an actor's ability to hear coaching and to correct his or her performance according to your instructions. It's good to cast coachable people, if you have a choice; unfortunately, if you haven't worked with a person before, you won't know how coachable that person is.

When you announce auditions, be sure to give enough description so that people know in general what the play's about. Have scripts available so interested people can sign them out and look over the script before the audition. Do not photocopy the play: Normally that's illegal.

There are various methods of auditioning, all designed to help you make a decision about the most qualified actors for the roles: you can ask your people to A) read parts in the actual script B) do mime or improvisations C) be prepared to read a monologue of their own choice. Professional directors use "C" more; nonprofessionals have traditionally relied on "A". I have increasingly found "B" to be valuable. I have my candidates read scenes together, trying people in various roles, but also I give them mimes to do ("fly a kite across the stage, see it get hung up in a tree, try to get it down, show how you feel about it!"). The mimes help me see how my auditioners handle themselves on stage and how self-conscious they are; also, the extent to which they can be creative with their bodies. All of this is important even if you're planning a mime-free show!

Remember, too, that poor readers can often act—so if you rely exclusively on "A" you will exclude a number of people who, once lines are memorized, may turn out to be splendid! And sometimes your excellent sight readers turn out to lack creative ability on stage.

A few assorted footnotes to auditioning . . . Let anyone read who is interested in a given role: Don't deny anyone a chance to read for a part he or she likes. And be gracious to those candidates you're cutting: Compliment them on what they did well, thank them for giving up a night for tryouts, and offer the reliable ones some other role on the production team!

The church director has a more difficult task than the professional director. You cannot call on an endless supply of talent from Central Casting until you find the precisely perfect actor for the role. You will be limited to a rather small pool, most of them female, which is problematic in that most of the roles in most plays are male. But you do the best you can, and when the job is done well the result will be its own reward.

Rehearsals, Blocking, Coaching

Once you have a cast, you the director need to set up a rehearsal schedule. As a rule of thumb you need about thirty hours of rehearsal for each sixty minutes of performance: A thirty-minute play would require about fifteen hours of rehearsal. Plan regular hours/days each week, with at least three rehearsals per week if possible. Rehearsals generally follow this pattern from Day 1 to performance: (a) reading (b) blocking (c) working (d) polishing (e) technical (f) dress rehearsals. Often, because of slow line-learners or other production snafus, working-polishing-tech rehearsal time gets condensed with much less time being spent polishing the play than is desirable.

The initial rehearsal is used for reading through the play with your cast and discussing its theme and characters. It may be helpful to ask each cast member to list five adjectives that are appropriate to his or her character: This provides a good basis for discussing characterization. The analysis can be extended by asking the actors to draw upon their memories for personal experience similar to that of their characters and to invent some central gesture (a physical mannerism, if you will) that seems appropriate to the character. All of this becomes the framework for developing a character who is credibly three-dimensional, not incredibly lackluster.

Blocking rehearsals are used for blocking the action. Make sure that your actors use *pencils* to write stage directions in their books as you give them. If you don't control this, half the actors will use pens (which is a problem if changes are made later) and the other half will just nod or say "I'll remember" and not write down anything! (They won't remember: They'll keep asking, "What was my direction here?")

For the benefit of your rookie actors, show them how a stage is divided:

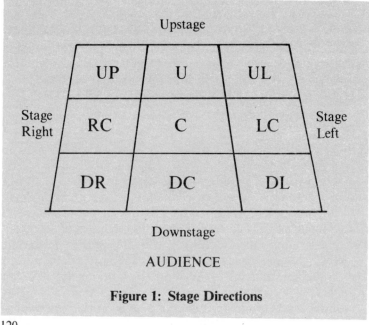

Figure 1: Stage Directions

As you explain that the stage is divided into areas, make sure your actors know that stage "right" and "left" are from the standpoint of the actor, not the audience. It helps if they know the history: Early renaissance stages sloped up from the apron to the scenic backdrop, so that actors were physically higher when upstage. With this understanding, explain how the actors can write down stage directions in shorthand: "Cross to downstage left, or down left," may be noted, "XDL," and "Cross to Mary at sofa" may be noted, "XMary/sf."

The stage diagram on page 120 is for a *proscenium* stage, one with the audience seated entirely in front. The stage directions would be similar for the *thrust stage*, where the audience is seated on three sides:

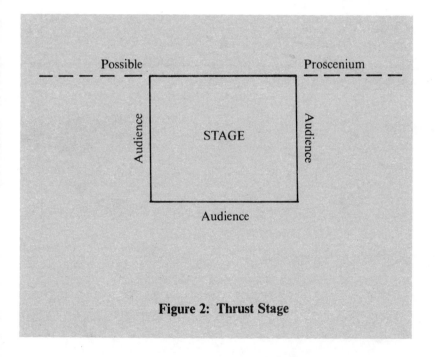

Figure 2: Thrust Stage

The thrust has the advantage of getting the audience closer to the action. The audience is involved even more closely with *arena staging*, where viewers sit on all four sides, or around the circumference of the playing area. The arena stage area has to be divided differently for blocking: Assume a clockface and think of the playing area in terms of hours. "Xto9"/ would mean "Cross to the nine o'clock position," etc.

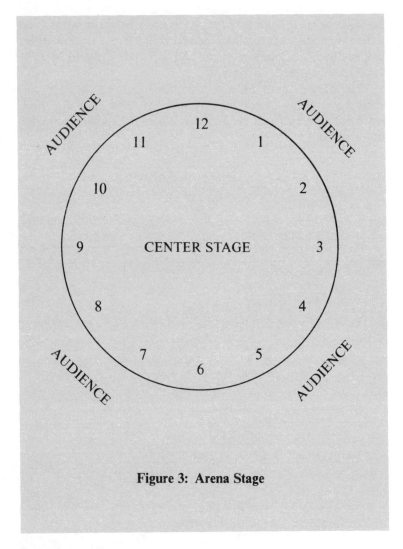

Figure 3: Arena Stage

Arena staging has the advantage of audience proximity, and in some ways a more natural style of acting; but of course the major disadvantage is that the arena stage prevents you from using any substantial scenery. Also, it may be harrowing for beginning actors: Their concentration may be distracted by having some spectators within their sight lines. But the arena often produces very exciting theatre.

Blocking needs to be carefully planned by the director prior to rehearsal. Changes can be made if some action doesn't work on stage, but the director who waits until he or she gets there to decide about blocking wastes everyone's time. In preparation, you may want to draw a large diagram of your stage plot, with whatever scenery and properties you're planning to use, and lay that diagram on a desk or table. Then take small cardboard squares, labeled with the characters' names, and move them about the diagram, making blocking notes in your playbook and drawing occasional diagrams in your book to indicate the stage picture at critical moments. Incidentally, most published playbooks are too small, the margins are cramped—so take the book apart and create a looseleaf notebook, alternating pages of the playscript with blank sheets of paper. Then you will have plenty of room to make blocking notes, as well as notes about costumes, lighting changes, etc., that correspond to the lines.

The director is the one who controls time and space to produce an arresting work of art. Blocking is the attempt to *control space*. The following general rules (there are often exceptions) apply to stage movement:

1. Keep your actors' faces open to the audience as much as possible. This means that as actors talk on stage they will usually stand in three-quarter position (halfway between a profile and frontal stance). This affects the total stage picture. For example, you normally wouldn't design your set with the jury placed up center in a courtroom drama because it would force your attorneys to turn away from the audience to argue before the jury.

2. If it is a naturalistic play, avoid having three or more actors stand in a straight line. In an abstract or stylized play, that may be effective. (Musicals tend to be stylized.)

3. When actors cross each other, they normally cross *in front* of another actor. Also, actors seldom or never *back up* on stage; they turn and walk directly to the next location, then turn again to face the appropriate character.

4. Often you need to give your central character in a particular scene some prominence. There are various ways of doing this: The character may be distanced from others, placed up center or downstage facing the audience (if appropriate), or elevated to a higher level by means of a platform, steps, a ladder, etc. If you

can manage to use two or more acting levels, this will add visual interest to your production.

5. Keep the stage picture in balance at least 80 percent of the time. The set should be balanced initially; that is, don't overload your props on one side of the stage. (It doesn't have to be a symmetrical balance, of course.) Actors, too, need to be kept in balance. It's important to provide *motivation* for any movement or business by an actor—it helps if they can understand why they're moving—but if the stage has to be balanced and you can't supply that motivation, move the actor anyway.

To be more specific: Don't put all your actors on one side of the stage for a long period of time. You can have one character stage left with five characters right if the one is more important or significant—or is delivering a harangue or threatening the others with a gun. And that character can chase the others from one corner of the stage to another, with them keeping enough distance to keep the stage in balance. This would be an asymmetrical balance, but still balanced.

Keep in mind also that when you have someone make a cross it will change the dynamics and throw the stage off-balance, if the actor doesn't return immediately. Others may have to move, or at least "cheat" a little to keep the stage balanced. (The term, "cheating," means that an actor makes a subtle movement—possibly taking one casual step right or left—to bring the stage back into balance or to keep him or herself in view of the audience, if blocked by downstage actors.)

Use specific movements to visually emphasize the dramatic action. Don't allow actors just to "stroll," and try to avoid aimless shuffling: Get them to keep their feet planted. Emphasize the point that nervous movement is distracting and weakens the character.

6. Prepare visually for entrances and exits. Clear the area around an entrance before an entrance. Place your entrances and exits in easily accessible areas. And unless you're planning to do a complete "box set," don't insist on having real doors—in abstract plays, actors can often just "appear." In more naturalistic ones, often the opening and closing of doors can be mimed or we can assume that the door was "opened" in the wings, out of sight of the audience.

7. Make sure the central character in a scene is the focus of attention, or the person or persons speaking at the moment. Be sure that the others are listening and watching the speaking

actor—or whoever is doing important business—and reacting to that speech or business . . . but don't let them react too strongly, so as to distract the audience.

8. Use each part of the stage wisely. Use the entire stage, but not all of it all the time.

Controlling *time* has to do with the rise and fall of tension leading to the major and minor climaxes. As a director you will need to control the tempo. Make the actors aware of the climaxes and tell them when they need to slow or pick up the pace.

During the working-polishing rehearsals, you will need to *coach* your actors; that is, suggest ways for them to improve voice projection, timing, stage business, line readings, and characterization. There has been a long debate in the theatre as to how actors should develop their characters. The *external* approach is to suggest that an actor observe people, copy their expressions and mannerisms (Moliere was unfairly accused of using a mirror to mimic Scaramouche), and try to reproduce those behaviors on stage; the acting-out will simulate the emotions well enough to make the character convincing. The *internal* or "method" school of acting, which relies on the techniques taught by the famous Russian director, Stanislavsky, attempts to evoke those feelings internal or natural to an actor that can be used to create a convincing character: The actor draws on his or her own experience for the raw material of the character.

Both approaches are viable, I think, and most of us are eclectic—we use whatever seems to solve a given problem. Christian directors are using theatre games and exercises more and more to assist actors in their stage business and characterization. For example, Warren Harris of Bethel College (Kansas) mentions two acting problems he had in doing Wilder's *The Long Christmas Dinner*, a play that relies heavily on mime and imagination: A character can age twenty years in ten minutes in this unique drama that telescopes time. The problems were the miming of eating and the rapid aging of characters.

My solution was to set aside a few hours of rehearsal for concentrated workshops on overcoming these problems . . . my method was to organize theatre games on "What Am I Eating?" until everyone developed a sense of the particular gestures and mannerisms related to the way we eat certain foods. Then the cast practiced the miming of eating while sitting around a table carrying on a conversation on subjects about which no one was likely to be at a loss for something to say, e.g., "Where were you when you heard that President Kennedy had been shot?" During this I side-coached when necessary to help the actors remember what they had discovered about the miming of eating.

A similar approach was used to make the actors aware of what gives us clues as to a person's age. This consisted mainly of playing, "How Old Am I?" in this way: Two teams were formed and each member tried to portray a different age range of ten to fifteen years. Then the other team guessed what age each was attempting. . . . Part of the game consisted of guessing by simply listening to the voices of people to whom one had his back turned.[3]

Similar games can be employed creatively during rehearsal to generate solutions and skills related to a variety of stage problems.

The question arises, should you interrupt an actor to work on a specific problem when a scene is moving along? I think it should be done, certainly during the early rehearsals. If an actor does something poorly without correction, such as misreading a line, that mistake will be reinforced. Kindly stop the action and correct the actor. Then run the sequence over to enable that actor to reinforce the correction.

By the way, there is stage business that is very difficult for beginning actors, especially shy or young people: the stage kiss, for example. In a college play I directed, one young man playing Judas had to kiss another actor on the cheek: Jesus. I never quite got that young man over his natural aversion to kissing another male! During rehearsals I let him get away with a weak hug and swipe at the other actor's cheek—it wasn't convincing—but when he said, "I'll get it right in performance," I believed him. I was wrong—performance came, and he did it the same way—unconvincingly! Make sure any difficult business is learned in rehearsal; otherwise it may never be done.

These are some common acting problems that may require coaching:

1. *The failure to learn lines.* There is no easy way to learn lines, although I've found that reading my cue lines into a tape recorder, adding silent space long enough for my own speeches, gives me a tape I can use over and over by myself to learn lines. It is also important to stress that your actors should learn their stage business and movement along with the lines: They can do this at home by moving the furniture about to suggest the stage set.

Emphasize that lines need to be learned early on so that everything else can be developed and polished.

2. *The failure to project lines audibly.* Actors with poor breathing will project a weak voice, and they need help on diaphragmatic breathing. (See exercises under Resources.) Often weak projection is a result of poor articulation and/or speaking too rapidly. Your coaching may include comments like, "Slow down, Joe, what's your hurry?" "Sharpen your consonants, Mary." "Take a breath or two every sentence, Bill." "Remember the back row!" Diction exercises will help. And try to sit in the back during an early rehearsal and then a later one—yell "Voice!" whenever anyone drops a line you can't hear. Beginners have to be reminded that while they seem to be speaking to the actors next to them on stage, they are really talking for the benefit of the entire audience—and so their conversation has to be much louder than normal.

3. *Failing to respond quickly to cues.* Nothing slows a show more than this. Church plays often drag because of that lag between speeches when actors are thinking, "Was that my cue? Well, my line is. . . ." Dialogue needs to flow smoothly as a rule, without so much as a one-second pause. There are times and places for "takes," "double-takes," and otherwise pregnant pauses; but for the most part actors should keep the pace up!

4. *Failing to act with the whole body.* Remind your more wooden actors (without insulting them) that there is a body below the neck, and use warmup exercises (see Resources) designed to loosen them from their inhibitions and become physically more animated. And remind them that on stage they're always involved: Even when someone else is giving a line, they need to be *reacting* physically to what is said and done. Of course, there is a fine line between reacting and *overacting*, which in its abuse becomes scene-stealing. In our college version of *The Gardener Who Was Afraid of Death*, some of the serious moments were "stolen" by the actor playing Second Soldier, who has very few lines but who slurped milk from his bowl and grunted and grimaced! He was in character but he was overdoing it, thus drawing attention from the main action.

5. *Dropping out of character.* Actors must be encouraged (prodded!) to stay in character the entire time they're on stage. Nothing frustrates a director more than the actor who won't take his or her role seriously, or who "cracks up" at every opportunity. I

was so frustrated by the antics of one college actor that after working with him in three plays I said, "Sorry, but please don't audition for the next play!" (He took it surprisingly well.)

After the blocking, working, and polishing rehearsals comes the technical, or "tech" rehearsal. Any scenery, lighting, sound effects, etc., that you intend to use in performance must be checked thoroughly in "tech" and cued to the appropriate lines and/or movement. Actors don't like "tech" much because they're standing around half the night, but it has to be done.

Finally, the dress rehearsal involves costumes and, if you're going to use it, stage make-up. Of course, any costumes that have a difficult feel to them, like petticoats and hoop skirts for women or armor and tuxedos for men, need to be tried on and tried out during earlier rehearsals. As actors work with special costumes it will help them feel their roles and get into character.

Keep everyone busy during rehearsal. Everyone who's called for rehearsal should be rehearsed or sent home. Actors shouldn't have to sit around. Those whose scenes are not being rehearsed on stage can perhaps rehearse with a prompter in another room; or they can be working on their lines so they're ready when needed. And make the rehearsals fun: Keep them moving, make them productive! Your cast will bless you!

As director, you need to be kind, yet firm. You need to be enthusiastic about the play and express confidence in your fellow artists! Expect the best, challenge your actors to do their best, and most likely you will get their best.

The Technical Side

So-called "tech" theatre consists of scenery and properties, lighting, costumes, makeup, and music or sound effects when used. Keep in mind that none of this is strictly necessary. The *sine qua non* for theatre is the actor; anything that distracts the audience from the interaction between characters is a no-no! When scenery and other technical effects are used sparingly and appropriately, they will enhance and support the action, not detract from it. We've all been put off by amateurish productions in which stage colors clashed, someone's costume was obviously wrong, or the lighting failed to illuminate faces within five feet of the apron. One is tempted on such occasions to say: Don't use any technical effects! But there is much to be said for the sage, careful use of scenic and sound effects.

128

Scenery and Properties

Scenery and properties together represent the visual stage picture, what is called the *set*. Scenery, or scenic backing, is the fixed element (although in Wilder's *The Skin of Our Teeth* it does shake at a critical moment in Act I). Properties are furniture and other portable items, including "hand props" like umbrellas, spears, or briefcases. Lacking a scene designer, the director will have to put the set together with what help is available; the stage manager may collect and place the properties, but sometimes actors can be assigned the task of bringing their own.

Interior sets (called "box sets" when they box in a single room) often consist of scenery laced together in the form of flats. A *flat* is a rectangular wooden frame across which muslin, canvas, or another paintable material is stretched. A good flat can be repainted and used over and over. Flats are connected and braced from behind and held down with weights, or lowered from fly-space on wires (in the more advanced theatres); constructed carefully, this can produce a very convincing set. However, many church groups will lack the interest or ability to build flats, since there is often little money and little space in which to build and store them. Incidentially, one good method of producing a landscape or another design on a flat is to make a transparency of the design and then throw it on the flat by means of an overhead projector. The image can then be drawn and painted on the flat.

Working without flats is fine, but I recommend that a church or college theatre group build or purchase certain scenic elements over time. Platforms and stair units can be used over and over. Everett Robertson recommends that you

> Construct portable lid and parallel units in 4' x 8' sizes, at 6" height intervals. For example, build two or three units 6" high, several more 12" high, and several 18" high. Then the 4' x 8' units can be stacked for additional height. Also, construct some 4' x 4' units that are 6", 12", and 18" high. Step units can be made to connect 12" or 18" intervals.[4]

As to properties: Stage furniture can be "borrowed" from other parts of the church, collected from auctions or rummage sales, from church members' attics, even from their living rooms! Directors often plunder their own homes, to their spouses' dismay: Once I used our dining room table and chairs in a campus

129

production of Thornton Wilder's *The Long Christmas Dinner*. It saved us some trouble and rental expense and, I'm happy to say, my wife was very understanding.

Most properties can be borrowed, bought, or rented. But there are some special items—armor, for example, or a chalice, a manger, or masks—that you may want to make yourself. There are many clever ways to use cloth- or papier-mâché, synthetic foams, cardboard, wood, fabrics, and cord to create convincing stage properties.

These methods are described in an excellent resource by Jacquie Govier, *Create Your Own Stage Props.*[5] Ms. Govier, using numerous diagrams, explains how to use and combine various materials to produce period properties: those of the classical Greeks, medieval people, etc., and including a section devoted to items used in nativity plays. Ms. Govier demonstrates, for example, how you can make stars, angel wings, and the manger from various materials; and how to produce masks from papier-mâché or plaster, using clay, sandmolds, or the actor's face. Creative masks representing people or animals can be produced from paper or from string dipped in glue and wound around a balloon. (And there is much more!)

Sometimes an idea that at first seems "stagey" or unconvincing turns out to work well: for example, the stage fire. Directing a historical scene in which infidels around St. Louis in the nineteenth century burned a stack of Bibles in front of a pioneer Baptist missionary, John Mason Peck, I considered various ways of making a stage fire. The solution came to me on a boat trip through the "Pirates Den" at Disneyworld, where some creative designing has been done. Hide a small fan and red spotlight behind the bonfired Bibles, tape colored strips of cellophane to a screen placed over the fan, turn the fan upward and, with the spotlight directed at the flying cellophane, you have a convincing illusion.

What about the curtain? Curtains are traditional, but no longer does anyone think they're indispensible. Curtains are used to open and close scenes, but you can use lighting to perform the same function by means of fadeouts and blackouts; it gives the audience time to reflect on the set before the action begins, which is psychologically good.

Here's another way to end a scene that I've found useful in directing a touring group which does a program of short sketches run in sequence, with narrative bridges. When we finish a sketch, the actors freeze for three seconds on the punchline, then turn in place toward the audience, and do a head bow. That lets the audience know we're finished without "milking" applause.

A final, unpleasant note regarding scenery and props. When the play is over the scenery must come down (Is this a good reason not to erect much scenery?), properties have to be returned, costumes need to be cleaned and restored to their rightful owners, and the performance needs to be evaluated. The director needs to take care of these things as soon as possible.

Lighting

Your performance area must be lighted, but stage lighting is not always necessary. Until about the sixteenth century virtually all theatre was performed outdoors, using God's own lighting; and when the first troupes moved indoors the house was lit with smelly candles, and later, foggy gaslights; neither could be raised or lowered in intensity. We have come a long way with our sophisticated, even computerized lighting systems today.

Lighting's main function is to illuminate the actors, but lighting has other functions as well: to open or end scenes; to create intensity or mood, especially by mixing colors; and to achieve special effects, as by means of blackouts, slow dims, cross-fading, backlighting, strobes, or scrim lighting.

In the short run, especially if you stay with liturgical drama, you can get along quite well without any lighting in addition to the standard house lights. But if you want to build a drama program you should probably add some special lighting. You can begin with PAR-lamps (150 watt bulbs) on alligator clamps, with barndoors to shield the light from the audience; but an ambitious group should plan to acquire a good lighting board (often called a "dimmer" or "scrimmer") and at least six good instruments.

Instruments include the standard fresnels, a general-purpose spotlight with at least a 500-watt capacity, or elipsoidal spotlights. The latter throw a sharp-edged spot as compared with the soft-edged spots of the fresnels. I would suggest that you plan to light your stage with at least five fresnels and one or two elipsoidals. Any of these instruments permit the use of color frames, or "gels," to produce different hues. Mostly you'll need ordinary white light with a bit of amber or pink to soften it. Avoid an overly generous use of strong colors, such as purple or orange, which will distort the actors and the scene.

Most colleges have decent dimmers. A church ought to purchase, in the long run, a good-quality dimming board with at least six dimmers, which would allow you to pair your lighting instruments or dim them separately. It ought to be portable—you may want to perform in several locations. You can purchase two or three lighting poles or "trees" that have heavy metal bases that can be set up anywhere to hold your fresnels. With good heavy-duty extension cords you'll be in business anywhere!

However, you should develop a "mainstage" inside the church where you can mount your lighting instruments. You might suspend a pipe or batten from the ceiling in the fellowship hall, to the front of the stage area, over the audience—make sure that it's far enough from the stage to provide a 45 degree angle when the instruments mounted on the batten throw light to the stage. Otherwise a part of the actors' bodies or faces will be poorly lighted when they are playing downstage.

The *scrim* is a special item that may be very useful to the busy theatre group. It's a lightweight fabric that is somewhat transparent when lighted from behind, creating a nostalgic or eerie effect—good for flashbacks or dream scenes. Also, the scrim can be used as a projection screen—it will take slides or movie images, thrown from either the front or rear. Rear projections are exciting when they produce scenic effects impossible to acheive with flats on a small stage. With a small proscenium stage (having no backstage space) you can use the scrim as the front curtain for rear projection, staging the main action in front of the proscenium closer to the audience. Scrims are expensive, however, even to rent. Consequently, some dramatists are projecting scenery on white walls or flats or on the back of the stage from projectors above the proscenium opening.

Makeup and Costuming

The point of using theatre makeup is to highlight the features of actors who are playing in strong light and/or at a great distance from the audience. Since these conditions usually do not prevail in the church, there I have found the use of stage makeup to be unnessary. Also, there is a tendency for non-professionals to use too much, and when it is liberally applied it can be distracting indeed. However, the special "character" face has to be made up: the old woman or man, for example, or the patriarchal face. For difficult makeups, like wigs and beards, actors should wear them in several rehearsals to get used to their new faces.

But *costuming* can never be left undone. Anything anyone wears in a play, except perhaps a birthday suit, becomes a costume. So it's important to think about how the play should be costumed, whether it requires a uniform apparel or something more individualized.

Some plays, particularly choric drama or ensemble performances, call for a uniform apparel, usually a neutral outfit like white or blue shirts and black trousers or skirts. Sometimes leotards and tights or trousers are worn for a neutral uniform, with other pieces—perhaps shirts, scarves, etc., added as needed. A college production of Turner's *Christ in the Concrete City* had the six actors in black leotards and white faces, and the actors carried swatches of thin, colorful material. As the chorus they would simply stand holding these swatches, which fell to the ground at their sides; as biblical characters in other scenes, they would drape them about their shoulders or heads to suggest biblical attire, or use them to suggest royalty (as Herod) or whatever.

Other plays call for individualized costumes, which may be period, modern, or abstract. Usually these are plays in which an actor plays a single character throughout. The characters themselves may suggest a certain dress due to age, position in life, or attitude. Such matters are probably more important than the period, although period costuming is often essential: One would not do a strictly biblical play in jeans, or even in bathrobes! But a more abstract play, or even a naturalistic drama from the nineteenth or early twentieth century wouldn't need to be strictly period. You can use modern dress, which may give it more application to our lives.

Take *Everyman*, for example, a medieval play which doesn't require medieval costuming. It's an abstract play, a statement about how to attain salvation, and it uses generalized characters such as Goods, Faith, and Confession. It can be costumed various ways. There was a television *Everyman* where it was set in an urban nightclub: Everyman wore a tuxedo.

If you want more abstract costumes, give some thought to what the characters represent: Goods, for example, might be cast as a heavy person (because the text speaks of Everyman's wealth as weighted down, unable to move) wearing a rich robe decked with fine jewels; or as a green-robed sequined figure held down by a pile of gold bullion; or as a fat bird (turkey) with dollar bill-like

133

feathers! The point is, although we have to be aware of the period in which a play was written or about which it speaks—costume the play, not the period!

For those doing strictly biblical plays, there is a brief, helpful discussion of costuming—with diagrams—in Robertson's *Introduction to Church Drama*. However, Lucy Barton's *Costuming the Biblical Play*[6] remains the standard work on the subject.

All of this means that someone must be responsible for costuming the production. Hopefully this person is skilled in tailoring or dress-making (not that he or she has to make all of the costumes!); also, skilled at prodding recalcitrant actors who defer the day of reckoning: "Don't worry, I'll find something in my closet!" This may be the right person to start a costume wardrobe for your drama group. Solicit contributions from people's attics, buy cheap apparel at thrift stores and sales, and especially be on the lookout for policemen's or military uniforms, doctors and nurses' outfits, and other specialized clothing. Build your wardrobe over time, lock it between performances, and make sure that everything's cataloged so you know what you have.

Looking Ahead

So you've finished a successful production: Why do a good play only once? Call around, solicit another performance or two. If it's portable, that is. (This may be another reason for keeping scenery light.) Perhaps another church will invite you to perform there, or agree to an exchange of productions.

But where do you go from here? I'd suggest you work with the pastor in developing a church drama committee. This committee becomes responsible for evaluating the most recent production, considering future plays, and planning drama for the church year. Planning a year's program, you need to think about the special needs and occasions in your parish or congregation. By way of example, a moderately ambitious year of drama might include . . .

1. Incorporating a short drama into worship once a month; a dramatic sermon at least once a quarter.

2. A special Maundy Thursday or Good Friday play. A passion play like Mueller's *Eyes Upon the Cross* would be a welcome relief on Good Friday from the endless repetition of sermons on "The Seven Last Words." A play about Judas, like Johnson's

Beloved Betrayer, would be appropriate on Maundy Thursday evening, as would Kenneth Barker's "The Last Meal," from *Dramatic Moments in the Life of Christ*.

3. Street theatre in connection with the social concerns committee, perhaps in connection with a peace emphasis.

4. A youth musical in cooperation with other community churches, perhaps for Thanksgiving or Pentecost.

5. Mission sketches to highlight a missionary emphasis or school of missions on Sunday evenings.

Many have found that an experimental worship or a coffeehouse setting are excellent opportunities for trying off-beat or informal drama, or what seems too "different" for tradition-oriented church members. At the church where I worship we used informal drama often during the seventies at an early service held at 8:30 a.m. Sunday mornings in the "Hall of Banners." George Ralph reports a similar experience at Hope Reformed Church in Holland, Michigan.

And the coffeehouse, a ministry begun by many churches and colleges during the sixties, seems an ideal place for provocative drama. Harry Farra of Geneva College has shared some ideas regarding coffeehouse dramas. The coffeehouse is a place where a Christian-secular dialogue often happens. But, he points out, "coffeehouses are often small, crowded, and noisy." You're playing in a difficult ambiance. A functional narrator may be useful, and it's better to rely on imagination than to attempt to rig sets in a coffeehouse. Short plays designed to stimulate discussion at the tables are best. Farra recommends such plays for coffeehouses as Mankowitz' *It Should Happen to a Dog*, Broughton's *The Last Word*, Albee's *The Sand Box* and *Zoo Story*, and Ionesco's *The Lesson*.

For additional help with planning the church year in drama, consult the helpful resources by Judy Gattis Smith[7] and by Miller and Dunlap.[8]

The Gift of Compromise and the Perils of Perfectionism

Eastman and Wilson began their fine manual on church drama with an introduction, "How to Kill Religious Drama." Tongue-in-cheek suggestions included:

Wish it upon the children. They did very well dramatizing a Bible story in a classroom, so of course they will know how to

135

produce an adult drama. . . . Turn it over to the choir director. He's a good fellow and will know how to handle the music. . . . If the choir director won't take charge of it, give it over to some nice young girl who once had a part in a high school play. . . . Provide no equipment for it. Instead, inspire the group to demonstrate what can be done under a handicap. . . .[9]

Facetious, of course. We are beyond many of those mistakes that church dramatists, venturing on an untried medium, formerly made. People are taking Christian theatre seriously these days.

But despite more training and available resources today, there is still the need for compromise. Maybe the new drama group can't find an experienced director—so there's a compromise. Maybe the Absolutely Right Play can't be found—so there's compromise. Perhaps too few of the most qualified actors try out for important roles—so there's compromise.

And if you've directed a play, you *know* there's no such thing as a Perfect Play Production: not with unreliable—and sometimes unrepentant—actors, lighting that fails when you need it, costumes that don't quite fit, or materials for that set that turn out to be unobtainable or extravagant. So you compromise between the ideal play you imagined and the practicality of the here and now, measured in terms of resources that are often limited and time that's always too short.

Be assured that some compromise is always necessary and that it doesn't make you a failure as director. Sometimes, in fact, a compromise yields a blessing in disguise. You may improvise a costume or make a stage property because you can't buy the materials you wanted, but the result turns out to be more convincing than you thought!

The same is true of the play as a whole: It will often turn out better than you imagined, despite the artistic shortcuts and compromising. After all, if it is the right play approached prayerfully, the Divine Spirit indwells it.

The result may be enlightening or inspiring, pleasing to the community of faith as well as to God, who is our ultimate auditor and arbiter.

8

Christian Street Theatre: Drama As Witness

Block parties, parades, festivals, Earth Day. Rummage sales, bake sales, sidewalk sales, and lawn parties. The streets are focal points of human activity: In warm weather people chat and gossip, gawk at unusual sights or attractive others, meet friends, flirt, giggle, banter, argue, enjoy life.

The first theatre we know was outdoor theatre. The great Greeks and the lesser Latins did their plays outdoors under the heavenly canopy. During the Middle Ages the streets became the routes taken by pageant wagons when they took their exciting mystery plays to the public. In our time, both secular and Christian groups have revived the ancient tradition of street theatre, bringing plays to many people who would never buy a theatre ticket and sit before the footlights, but who become enthralled by performances staged in their own neighborhoods and connected to their own experience. Street theatre speaks to them, not to the elite but the common folk, the people of the ordinary homes and gardens, the row houses, the "projects," and even the down-and-out, the hardened, hapless people of the metropolis.

Street theatre became very popular with ethnic groups and so-called radicals during the boisterous sixties when young people especially used it as an avenue of dissent and protest. Street theatre wasn't then and isn't now an *escapist* art but instead, *theatre of relevance*: It spoke to the problems and concerns of

137

certain classes, the poor, minorities, students disturbed by the war in Southeast Asia. One advantage of playing to a relatively unsophisticated audience is that since the spectators are not veteran theatre-goers, they have no built-in expectations regarding the performances. Older theatre conventions may be abandoned; almost anything goes, in other words, on the street, provided that everyone can hear and see the action.

Street theatre is message theatre. Roger Furmer of the New Heritage Theatre spoke of the dynamic of street theatre in the early seventies (*Theatre Crafts*, March/April 1972): "Growing up in a black community means we must take a special message out into the streets. It goes beyond just sheer entertainment. I feel our theatre definitely has to become a theatre of teaching. It has to say something directly to our people. I know that when we do scripts about the enemy—be it the landlord, the housing authority, or whomever—people truly respond because it touches them."

Christians might not use the term "enemy" to describe the targets of social protest, as Furmer does, (although we are warned of "principalities and powers" and the minions of Satan) but there are obstacles and adversaries in society, surely, that Christian love needs to confront in order to produce a more just and livable world. Street theatre may touch these issues and address these adversaries. It is indeed didactic theatre, but more; often it goes beyond edification and instruction—it attempts to provoke an audience to action.

Street theatre was popular in the sixties and early seventies, when groups like the San Francisco Mime Troupe and the Bread and Puppet Theatre, with its 25-foot puppets nearly scraping the sky, appeared on many campuses and in communities where the agenda was social change. Street theatre even came before the Supreme Court of the United States in 1967.

Two persons had performed an anti-war street theatre piece in front of the Armed Forces induction center in Houston, Texas. One of them, Daniel Schacht, wore an army uniform to symbolize the presence of the military in Vietnam. He was arrested and convicted of violating federal laws against the unauthorized wearing of a military uniform in a theatrical production intended to discredit the armed forces. However, the Supreme Court reversed, holding that the Constitution protected street theatre performers and that performances critical of the military are just as fully protected as favorable ones—an important First Amendment victory.

Although Christians began using street theatre during the sixties, many have left it for indoor theatres during the past decade. Still, street theatre, whether it is a relatively safe, prearranged performance or an abrasive, troubling sketch that surprises an audience, has great potential for Christian witness. We need to look at what's possible and positive about Christian street theatre.

There are biblical precedents. God told Isaiah to go naked and barefoot for three years as a warning to Egypt and Cush that they would be conquered by Assyria (Isaiah 20:1-4); and Jeremiah was instructed to put a yoke about his neck and thus to demonstrate God's warning to the nations, that if they did not submit to Nebuchadnezzar, King of Babylon, God would not preserve their lands or themselves (Jeremiah 27). Weren't these powerful symbolic statements? Indeed, Isaiah and Jeremiah were being asked to perform "monodramas" of warning.

In an earlier chapter we examined Ezekiel's use of a "brick" or slate as backdrop for a play predicting a dire event, the imminent siege of Jerusalem (Ezekiel 4:1-3). It was a teaching play, and a warning as well. Today, Christians are using drama to teach and to warn people about personal and social sins of the flesh and the spirit.

Modern Christian Street Theatre

Although it is not as active currently, the street theatre ministry of the Lamb's Players has probably been the most durable of any American professional group—and certainly the most evangelistic. The troupe was founded by Steve Terrell, who studied street theatre on a sabbatical at Berkeley in 1970. Terrell founded a troupe in Minneapolis, then moved it to San Diego in 1972 to take advantage of a warmer climate. Terrell's reason for founding The Lamb's Players was Christian outreach: "I was frustrated with catching a few sinners as they wandered into a church. I wanted to get out to the marketplace."

Although Terrell left the group after twelve years as its director, the Lamb's Players continue. They have added a mime troupe, readers' theatre, and a puppet troupe to the original street theatre productions, and they have secured an indoor stage as well.

In England a significant ministry developed in connection with St. Michael-le-Belfrey Church in York: first the Breadrock

139

Troupe and then the professional Riding Lights Theatre Company. Murray Watts and Paul Burbridge argue in their book of sketches, *Time to Act*, that street theatre "is one of the most dynamic forms of communication. It has immediate dramatic impact or not at all. An obscure subject, loose timing, inadequate staging, a fluffed line, all can lose an audience. But a confident performance of a good piece of street theatre can grip the attention of a crowd longer than the most talented performer at Hyde Park Corner."[1]

The Riding Lights Theatre Company specialized in short sketches, generally scriptural, comprising a program of twenty to thirty minutes, which the organizers felt was plenty long enough to hold an audience outdoors. The street theatre developed by the Lamb's Players ran somewhat longer, but the program was a single one-act play instead of a series of sketches. Initially Steve Terrell developed two shows for the street, both with Medieval period costuming and sets, which were highly visual and effective outdoors. One, *The Hound of Everyman*, was an updated version of the Medieval morality; the other, *Hark! the Ark!*, was a contemporized version of the account of Noah.

In street drama, the visual dimension takes precedence over the verbal-auditory dimension. "Talky" plays don't work unless they're backed by mime, music, or frequent gags. Pantomime is useful outdoors: Mimed action can be seen more readily than words may be heard. Even when lines are spoken, actors need to be coached to use their bodies more than usual, to make grand gestures, to be almost melodramatic. Burbridge and Watts contend that a show should be designed and presented in such a way that spectators will be able to tell what's happening even if they can't hear all the lines. In addition to mime, costuming and sets will add to the visual spectacle. The Lamb's Players' sets are large and colorful (large backdrops mounted on a platform) and they command attention. With a bare stage—no sets—costuming becomes more critical.

Outdoors, people are constantly moving; the crowd at a shopping center, for example, is always in flux. But with a good location and effective technique it is possible to hold an audience for at least a half hour.

You will need to find a location where people are loitering or relaxing, not in a hurry to move on. Perhaps the village square, a beach, a park, or a picnic grove near a factory at lunchtime would be the ideal site. More than one church, located in a downtown area, has used its own property for drama: The church front may be a meaningful backdrop, and the front steps may be used to enhance the vertical staging of scenes. After the 1962 consecration of the new cathedral at Coventry, England, a series of plays was presented on the cathedral porch, a church front with steps that were roofed over, ideal for inclement weather; and since it was adjacent to a pedestrian walkway through town, it was possible to hook an audience at lunchtime for a twenty-minute presentation.

Many church groups need to find more "secular" locations for outdoor performance. Again, it must be a place where people are relatively relaxed and unhurried. For this reason a bus stop would not do, unless the program were extremely short—people are "stuck" at a bus stop, but only for a brief interval. Beaches, parks, playgrounds, and public malls are probably better locations. If the property is publically owned, you may need to secure a permit; if it is privately owned, permission from the owner. It is courteous to inform the local police that you expect to draw a crowd at that location, even if you're performing on church or private property. By the way—as Steve Terrell points out, campuses, military installations, and prisons are excellent locations for Christian theatre—of course, in the latter two cases, and especially the last, you have a captive audience!

Use a combination of visual elements and sound to draw a crowd: colorful properties, a painted ladder, a freestanding door; actors wearing outlandish costumes, jumping rope, juggling balls, handing out balloons, sitting on each others' shoulders, whistling, playing kazoos or musical instruments. Presenting beach drama in Maine one summer with senior high conferees, we simply walked through groups of sunbathers, banging a huge oriental gong and announcing that a dramatic performance would begin momentarily on a lined-off space on the sand, facing the ocean.

The Lamb's Players often precede their street drama with a parade, consisting of horn players, a drum beater, and someone shouting the invitation to all and sundry for a free performance of "Hark! the Ark!" Meanwhile, back at the stage, one of the actors is doing a pre-show to hold the early-to-arrive spectators, perhaps a bit of juggling or mime. One thing the "welcomer" must do, according to Terrell, is try to bring the audience as close to the stage as possible (which is important even in the chancel, but especially outdoors). Auditors will be reluctant, perhaps suspicious of what's happening, but it's important to bring the audience close to the stage in order for them to hear everything, and to establish a strong rapport between actors and audience.

Burbridge and Watts found, working with British audiences, that "most people will come when some kind of performance has started," so they began with music—songs with a strong contemporary feel, jazz, reggae, spirituals, definitely not traditional church music. "Following this the first sketch . . . should be fast-moving, funny, and short. The next sketch should follow without a break: in other words, a good continuity man will link from sketch to sketch briefly and to the point, welcoming everybody to the show and perhaps saying something about the group, inviting the audience to any other events that might interest them and providing that all-important thirty-second gap for two of your actors to struggle out of Wild West costumes and get into Bill and Ben outfits!"[2] Their program moves from fast and funny stuff to a more serious Christian message, and then finishes with a bit of closing humor—the humorous, warm ending leaves the audience relaxed, and willing to stay and talk.

Burbridge and Watts have included a number of street theatre sketches in *Time to Act*. The one they suggest has had the greatest impact is called "The Light of the World," for a maximum cast of ten actors. (I have found it takes a minimum of five.) There is a narrator telling the story of Christ in a modern paraphrase of the gospel, with a drumbeat and rhythm and two groups of characters miming sins, etc., and the figure of Jesus, who is forced to mount a ladder as the crucifixion is reenacted. It is short, pithy, and powerful—ending with a strong challenge to the audience to become disciples of Christ.

Steve Terrell has done very different material with the Lamb's Players, but he agrees on the basic technique: Street theatre should be loud, fast, and funny. Terrell emphasizes humor more than Burbridge and Watts. He admits to including at least three "gags" on each page of street theatre dialogue. As you can see from this piece of "*Hark! the Ark!*", the gags are often corny but effective in warming up an audience and keeping them involved. Here Terrell has Gabriel appear to Noah:

GABRIEL: Could you tell this wandering wayfarer where I might find a man named Noah?
NOAH: Prithee, are you a bill collector?
GABRIEL: Well, you might say that.

142

NOAH: In that case, then, I don't know him.

GABRIEL: Permit me to introduce myself. My name is Gabriel, and I'm from the heavenly gates.

NOAH: Listen, if you're a salesman from that cemetery, I told the last one I'm not interested in burial plots.

GABRIEL: You don't understand, sir. I come from upstairs.

NOAH: "Upstairs!" Say, I'm sorry for that noise the other night, but that was my grandfather. You see, he lives with us and he's always having a wench over for a little drink. You know how it is . . .

GABRIEL: Nooo—I don't.

NOAH: *(Giving him a weird look)* Well, it got out of hand. I mean, at 969 you'd think—

GABRIEL: I'm an angel.

NOAH: Swell, I've got a friend down the street who raises Cain.

GABRIEL: What's his name?

NOAH: Adam.[3]

And so it goes, with slapstick and vaudeville humor, takes and double-takes, and mugging for the audience. But the Medieval costumes and the lavishly decorated set suggesting an ark captivate the audience immediately and listeners are held by skillful acting. And lest the message be lost in the somewhat fictionalized Old Testament story, at the end of "*Hark! the Ark!*", having defied the sheriff and the authorities who wanted to close down his building project, Noah steps on board the ark and the rain begins to come—with the help of a thunder sheet and wind-and rain-making machines; and the sheriff and mayor are aghast. After the family's on board, the authorities sputter off—and a huge curtain falls from the railing of the ship's deck onto an empty stage. On it is embossed, in a careful gothic hand:

> Without faith it is impossible to please God, for he who comes to God must believe that He is, and that He is a rewarder of those who seek Him. For God loved the world so much that He gave His only Son Jesus so that those who will commit themselves totally to Him shall not perish but have eternal life.

But the Lamb's Players feel that the most important thing happens after the play is over. Then cast and crew spread through the audience—except for one person delegated to guard the stage properties—looking for conversations and witnessing to their faith in Christ. Sometimes decisions are made; often seeds are sown that result in decisions later. Sometimes it is the excellence of the acting or the artistry of the set that initiates conversation. A theatre buff comes up to inquire about the set construction, which leads to dialogue with one of the production crew. "I can't get over Christians doing such quality work!" is typical. Or, "You people are really artists!"

Such conversations are important if your purpose is evangelism. If your troupe is timid about witnessing in public, you may want to take them through a workshop on witnessing, in which you role-play and discuss ways of talking about life and faith with a stranger. Or it may help to hand out tracts to trigger conversations; or, instead of conversation, simply hand out tracts or Bible portions to spectators as they are leaving.

Now, a word about mechanics: How do you make street theatre portable? The Lamb's Players have used a stage consisting of several 4' x 4' plywood platforms that are seated, on location, in a metal frame—having been carried there on a bus or van. The stage is heavy and requires some muscle to set up but is quite playable, with its 8' x 8' or possibly 8' x 12' area. Mobile-home jacks are used at the four corners to keep the stage level, for at any location the ground may be uneven.

Other ways of carrying and staging street drama are possible. Some groups have used flatbed trucks to carry the set as well as for performance space; others have used a converted school bus, or a pre-fab foldout trailer-stage. Some groups carry no stage platform but instead perform at street level, or on a hillside, on the steps in front of a public library or museum, or on the porch or portico of a building.

Guerrilla Theatre

There are two main kinds of street theatre. One uses a prearranged location and possibly even advance publicity to draw a crowd, as we have seen with the Lamb's Players; the other, with no warning, surprises people who happen to be in a particular location, and who are perhaps made into spectators against their will. We may call the latter, *guerrilla theatre.*

The term is borrowed from guerrilla *warfare*, which is a hit-and-run series of engagements usually enacted by small bands of soldiers against a superior force. The tactics include surprising the adversary, a quick encounter, then escape. Similarly, guerrilla theatre is often performed by small bands who surprise people, instantly creating an audience, and then escape—usually leafletting the crowd in the process. Guerrilla theatre tends to make viewers uncomfortable. There is no real "enemy" present but spectators become the targets of persuasion—the sketch is designed to provoke a response or present an alternative point of view which may offend some viewers and galvanize others.

My work with beach drama in Maine was borderline guerrilla theatre. We did assemble an audience of people who were surprised to find us on the beach, and we used no prearranged locations—and then we performed quickly and moved on. But our sketches were not abrasive in tone but, rather, thoughtfully evangelistic. Certainly we didn't offend anyone.

But there is a place today for an *offensive* guerrilla theatre. Jesus calls us to address the vital issues of the world, to speak against indignities such as poverty, hunger, unfair working conditions, and discrimination, as well as the threats posed to human life by abortion, pollution, acid rain, and nuclear weapons. To be sure, these issues are controversial: You will find both "pro-life" and "pro-choice" Christians, for example. But certainly we must examine these issues, conduct research, discuss them prayerfully, and try to agree on the position that Jesus would take. Then we need to find ways of bringing the issue to the public's attention or changing policy on it. Drama can do these things: It is a consciousness-raising tool.

Like Isaiah's nakedness and Jeremiah's yoke, a single actor may be sufficient to present a critical issue. Someone locking herself into a contaminated cell may protest the dangers of working in a particular chemical factory, or an individual staggering under the weight of an enormous nuclear missile (cardboard or papier-mâché chained to his back will clearly demonstrate the burden of arms spending and the threat of nuclear war. Or, an individual chained to the door of the IRS office on April 15 might be expressing outrage on one of several issues. The issue would be identified by an adjacent sign: "Don't Pay Taxes for War," or "Don't Subsidize Apartheid," or "Don't Finance U.S. Intervention in the Third World!" These mini-dramas would each call attention to a perceived injustice.

Once a Christian fellowship has studied an issue and prayed, seeking God's will and coming to a conclusion about the stance they need to take, then they are ready to brainstorm possible scenarios to dramatize their message. Having chosen a sketch and having rehearsed it and decided on a presentation in a certain place, the group is ready to perform. The result may not be the best Christian art—for we have a kind of propaganda play—but the group is legitimately using drama to serve Jesus Christ.

There are some caveats. You need to avoid spiritual arrogance, which is the assumption that your position is the *only* possible stance; and you try to be quite sure that God wills this particular action at this time. In terms of tactics, you have to avoid blocking pedestrian or vehicular traffic, and in general you ought to be sensitive to the needs of businesspeople on the street or in the mall. A performance that held up traffic or blocked a parking lot for fifteen minutes might be inappropriate; but I say only, *might* be, for you may be able to conceive of a cause so immediate and so incredibly important that it would justify some temporary (if not permanent) inconvenience to pedestrians and drivers.

In planning a surprise performance on the street, keep in mind that your audience may be confused and distracted, so your sketch needs to be very pointed, loud, and visual—short goes without saying. Having finished, you need to leaflet the crowd and move on to another location, perhaps at the next intersection. Leafletting is critical since the noise and distractions may have prevented the audience from hearing spoken lines. The leaflet, which should look professional, will explain the protest, giving some background on the issue and indicating how people can act on it themselves.

To illustrate further, let's consider the position that many Christians are taking on nuclear weapons, that—in brief—since ours is a God of life, not death, and since Jesus taught us to love our enemies, not destroy them, nuclear weapons cannot be justified. Virtually everyone deplores their use in warfare. But many Christians hold as well that even the manufacturing or possession of weapons of such megadeath potential has to be condemned as a sin against God and a potential crime against humankind. Taking such a position, here are three potential guerrilla theatre scenarios:

1. Someone dressed as the Grim Reaper, with one arm hugging a huge cardboard missile inscribed with the U.S. and U.S.S.R. symbols, silently greets pedestrians and hands them leaflets as they pass.

2. a) Pallbearers dressed as nuclear missiles carry a casket

146

bearing a huge globe, to the beat of a funereal drum, bells, and/or funeral march hummed on kazoos or wailed on bagpipes. Or, b) the pallbearers on one side wear red shirts with Soviet emblems, those on the other side wear red-white-and-blue outfits with American emblems—but what they carry, like a casket or battering-ram, is a huge nuclear missile. A third group of actors runs in front of the missile to stop it, waving their arms frantically; but they are mowed down as the "pallbearers" walk all over them. The protesters get up, run around in front, and try again, but they are repeatedly mowed down as the "parade" continues.

3. Let's have two groups of actors, perhaps on opposite sides of the street, and two huge missiles. One side's waving American flags and the other's waving Soviet flags. They shout insults and attempt to fire their missiles; but the missiles topple and squash the people who attempt to use them. Posters are then raised proclaiming that "Those Who Live by the Sword Will Die by the Sword," with the word "sword" crossed out and "missile" written in above. Or the peace movement favorite might be used, "End the Arms Race—Not the Human Race." Again leaflets may be used, providing information about, for example, a specific arms control or test ban bill currently facing Congress.

None of the foregoing scenarios enlists the spectators physically. Let me suggest a non-abrasive sketch that does. Take three large glass jars with you to a public place, along with a wad of dollar bills. You need four people, one for each jar and one to dispense the money.

The first jar is held by someone wearing a physician's coat or a nurse's uniform, and is labeled "Human Services." The second is held by someone wearing an eyeshade or something to suggest an accountant, and is labeled "Federal Deficit." The third, held by someone in military fatigues, is titled, "The Military." When a pedestrian comes along, the fourth person awards him/her a dollar bill and asks that it be placed in the pedestrian's favorite federal budget category. (Handing people money gets their attention!) The pedestrian is forced to make a choice.

A peace group in Kansas City using this technique found that the Human Services jar filled up faster than the others, and the Military was a distant third. Pedestrians were given a leaflet explaining how the federal budget is allocated and showing how it is weighted heavily toward the military. This was a useful way of sensitizing people to the discrepancy between our Christian values and federal budget allocations.

These scenarios are merely a sample of those you might consider for this particular issue. Granted, they seem simplistic. The question of national defense is complicated but if one sees nuclear weapons (and not the Soviet Union) as the principle threat to our security, indeed to that of humankind, these sketches are relevant. Indeed, in the light of our call to be peacemakers this sort of guerrilla theatre seems eminently Christian.

Doing such drama makes you vulnerable, of course. You need to be prepared for hostile reactions, even jeers and insults. (We've been warned of that in Matthew 5:11-12.) You will need to assess an action in terms of whether enough of your audience is "turned off" by the performance to make it counter-productive. But even if some are hostile, you may be sowing the seeds of change as people who were surprised or shocked by an "offensive" theatre piece go home distressed and disturbed . . . and *thinking.*

Conclusion

Street theatre is fun. Painting sets for a Lamb's Players-like production in a public park, conversing with patrons after a show and sharing faith with them, or performing troubling sketches about abortion, pollution, hunger, farm workers' rights, or nuclear weapons are exciting and enjoyable ways of witnessing.

Street theatre can be a marvelous ministry. It is a witness to God's truth as you understand it. It is making the invisible visible. It is an acting out of faith.

Yours.

9

Playwrighting

If the Absolutely Right Play doesn't appear, you have to compromise between what you want and what's available. If this happens time after time, compounded by the fact that those scripts you order from catalogs seldom live up to their glowing descriptions, there is an answer—write your own plays.

Not everyone can do this—Thornton Wilder, himself both novelist and playwright, said that writing for theatre is the most difficult literary art—but more people can write plays than think they can. God gave us creativity with *imago dei*; for if God is our maker, and we are made in his image, we must have some talent for *making*.

Notice, the word is *playwright*, not play*write*. A wainwright makes wagons, a shipwright makes boats, and a playwright makes plays. To say play*write* implies that the writing of words is all; but that is not all. A written play is but ink squibbles on paper until it is mounted on a stage and the words are spoken by performers acting before an audience. Remember, theatre is a "seeing place," so playwrighting is a shaping or crafting of something that is audio-visual and meant for an audience.

In *St. Joan*, George Bernard Shaw's heroine is informed by skeptics that the voices she hears come from her imagination. "Yes," she answers, "that is how God speaks to me." Imagination is the doorway to faith as well as to creativity. God speaks through the imagination of the artist, be it painter, sculptor, or playwright—to stimulate the imagination of the viewer.

Considering Your Stage and the Audience

Writing for a church, community, or college theatre is quite different from writing for the commercial stage. The professional writer has fewer restraints: the wizardry of flying scenery, electronic staging, and computerized lighting enable him or her to conjure up marvels at a wink. But for the nonprofessional there are usually no trapdoors in the stage, no fly space, no turntables, no backlighting, no scrim, and no strobes. As Paul T. Nolan says in an excellent short primer, *Writing the One-Act Play for the Amateur Stage*,[1] "Anything written for the amateur stage should require only those stage effects that can be accomplished in an empty room," and he makes a good case for using only a single, simple stage set. Of course, set changes are made easy by the use of *suggestive* scenery as opposed to a naturalistic set. A suggestive set would have just a picket fence, a well, or a porch swing against a neutral background—or, if interior, just two or three pieces of furniture to represent a living room. In *Happy Journey to Trenton and Camden*, Thornton Wilder had four kitchen chairs represent an automobile. Sets can be changed rapidly, using suggestive scenery with nothing lost; in fact, the audience's imagination may be stirred!

Writing for a Christian audience is different from writing for a non-Christian or mixed audience. Churchgoers come expecting to be edified or inspired and they will accept a moral more easily than a secular audience will. Also, the secular audience is less likely to see the Bible as an authority and may be skeptical about themes based on biblical material.

The language is different too. A secular audience may refer to religious terms like "born again" as "God-talk," and find it unacceptable; on the other hand, profanity which a secular audience takes for granted would not go down in church. This is both good and bad. The Christian playwright doesn't want to poison a profound message with offensive language or take the Lord's name in vain, but there are characters and settings which are not credible without some rough language: You wouldn't expect a stevedore to talk like a nun. Fortunately, we don't have to write many plays about stevedores.

Ways to Begin

So how do you begin writing a play? Probably you begin in one of four ways:

1. With a *story* that seduces you. There is nothing immoral or illegal in "borrowing" a story from someone. The Greeks, Shakespeare, every major playwright did it. Today the copyright law specifies that *ideas* cannot be copyrighted, only the *form* in which they're expressed. Mortals find it impossible to be entirely original. They use ideas the human race has developed over time. Think of it as recycling ideas that belong to humanity.

So where do you get the stories? From the Bible, of course, but also from history, newspapers, your own experience, and anecdotes told by friends . . . even comic strips and cartoons!

2. With a *theme* or premise that compels you: repentance and resurrection, stewardship, love, integrity, social concern. You should be more specific: Christian stewardship of the environment, integrity in the face of peer pressure to use drugs, or social concern in terms of helping to integrate a conflict-ridden, prejudiced neighborhood. But beware: Your play can become moralistic if your premise dominates the characters. The problem with beginning with a premise is that the play may turn into a sermon.

3. With a *character* that intrigues you. Plays have been written about popes and princes, kings and commoners, politicians and saints. Turning famous people into protagonists has become an art form, and plays about Buffalo Bill, Sir Thomas More, Galileo, Gandhi, Emily Dickinson, and others attest to their success. These days Hollywood and the television networks consume material voraciously, hardly waiting for a celebrity to expire before running a docu-drama on the individual.

4. With a *situation* that interests you. Personally, I like fantasy: a prenatal soul awaiting birth or a psychotic who thinks he's Jesus, or Judas. From these two bizarre situations I've spun out several short plays. But it doesn't have to be fantasy. If you take an interesting location and introduce conflict or confrontation you have a dramatic situation. There are many dramatic situations in the Bible that haven't been thoroughly exhausted by playwrights (although perhaps by preachers!); and many in contemporary life.

Suppose a father comes backstage after watching his daughter perform for the first time on a professional stage. What happened on stage? Why is he there? How does he react? Perhaps she believes her performance to have been a failure and he reassures her; that's not terribly dramatic. But if he is critical of what she thought was a successful performance there will be conflict. Perhaps she has taken a role he doesn't approve of; perhaps he has come to remove her forcibly from an occupation he finds offensive; or perhaps he begs her to return home because her mother/ brother/sister is dying. She isn't sure whether this is a ruse to get her away from the theatre; she leaves him on some pretext and calls home to find her mother well; she returns to have it out with her father. A simple setting, to begin—but its dramatic potential is endless.

Developing Your Drama

Whether you begin with a story, premise, character, or situation, you will be adding the other elements eventually; otherwise you have no play. But once underway, how do you continue and what are the key elements?

There are many ways to write a script. Some like to establish a setting and characters and start writing dialogue; they believe in "giving the characters their head." If it works, the play almost writes itself! Others prefer to outline the play first before writing any dialogue. The outline then becomes a *scenario* or *plot*. This has value because if you know how your play's going to end you have something to work toward.

Plays are built around a central action, either an external, physical action or something internal like the terrible decision the early Christian Phocus has to make, in *The Gardener Who Was Afraid of Death*: Shall he reveal his identity to the Roman soldiers who are looking for him? But usually the action is external and physical. When you're describing a play you've seen, a friend will inevitably ask, "But what *happens?*"

Indeed, something must happen. The point at which the excitement peaks is called the point of crisis, or *climax*. To put it differently, the rising action usually peaks with a momentous decision, a *choice* that Thomas A. Becket or Sir Thomas More or Judas or Jesus or Phocus has to make; or, alternatively, with a *response* made by others to an action taken by the protagonist— Captain Vere to Billy Budd, the religious court to Joan of Arc at her trial. In these cases we want to know what the sentence is and how the protagonist will respond to it. The climax is followed by the denouement. Clearly the falling action must be relatively brief; otherwise it will be an anti-climax.

Characters take many forms. But if you're writing a serious message-play with a contemporary setting, you want to people your stage with psychologically credible characters. They need to be three-dimensional and "real" enough for spectators to identify with them. You need to study people carefully with a biologist's eye, then write notes on what you've seen and what you surmise. Take ordinary or extraordinary people, examine them, expand them slightly for the stage, and you have the makings of a serious drama; expand them broadly and you have a silly farce, perhaps, or a searing social satire.

You may be led, especially if your play is presentational or stylized, to use a *functional* character. This person functions as mediator between stage and audience; he or she may be the author's spokesperson, commenting on the action, introducing scenes, etc. The Greek chorus functions collectively this way; so does Wilder's Stage Manager in *Our Town*, and Sabina in *The Skin of Our Teeth*. Such a device breaks down the illusion of distance, narrows the gap between stage and audience. It may be useful to have one or more characters speak to the audience directly, either as interpreters of the action or simply to give humorous "asides."

Even if you didn't begin with a premise, your play will have a central idea, or theme. Resist the temptation to express your theme baldly in the lines. This may be as inartistic as "for an artist to paint a picture of Christ on the cross and then draw a circle extending from his mouth and put in that circle the Seven Last Words."[2] Hopefully your premise is expressed in the play's action; it may be seen through the prism of behavior, that of your central character or others. Shakespeare doesn't *talk* about jealousy in *Othello* but *shows* how jealousy can destroy both the innocent wife and her husband. Chapman and Coxe, following Melville, don't talk about the power of innocent suffering in *Billy Budd* but show it through the brutality of the Master at Arms inflicted on the young seaman, and the effect of the young sailor's character on his shipmates.

Write tentatively. It may be a mistake to put everything in print too early—you may get locked into an idea that's inferior to something God may show you later. Just brainstorm ideas prayerfully, write them all down, and see how they fit together. Then

153

write dialogue. And when you're finished you may not be. Play-wrighting is re-wrighting.

I keep a file of ideas in various stages of development, from raw to half-baked to almost-edible! When I return to that file to rework a particular notion it's like meeting an old friend, and at that point I'm often amazed at how I can see the dramatic problem differently, and with more intelligence. Often we need to wait upon the Spirit for days, weeks, or years.

So you think you have a decent first draft? Although it is out of print, Fred Eastman's *Writing the One-Act Religious Play* contains some excellent "Tests for Your Completed First Draft." File your draft away for a few days, then dig it out and try to read it objectively, as if it were not your own (very difficult to do, but important). Then check it against some standards. These are Eastman's questions about dramatic structure (without his elaborations):

I. Does it have the necessary dramatic strength?
  1. Does it reach the emotions?
  2. Do the characters seem real?
  3. Is the conflict adequate?
  4. Does the conflict rise to a climax?
  5. Is the suspense sustained?
  6. Do the characters have to make important choices?
  7. Is the theme clear and worthwhile?
  8. Is the solution convincing?
  9. Does the play reveal a struggle common to the experience of the audience?
  10. Does the play present contrasting moods?
  11. Does it have a well-knit episodic stucture?[3]

About Endings

Recently I've read two short works on playwrighting. Both were very clear about ways and means of beginning, both very vague on endings. Often our dramas are over-written; we don't know when to stop, so we keep on writing. It is much better to leave the audience wishing there had been more, than wishing the play had finished sooner!

The ending of a one-act play—and that is mostly what Christian playwrights are producing—*should have a bite to it.* It may

154

not "sting" like a stinger, but it will challenge and confront an audience in some way; or the final lines will leave the spectators pondering and wondering, or thinking about how it all relates to their own lives. In my play, *Immediate Delivery* (formerly "The Waiting Room,") which involves four prenatal souls awaiting birth, and with the power to choose not to be born—and confused by interaction with a newly-dead "Butcher" who is angry about the life he's just finished and the state of things on earth and an "Angel" who tries to put the best face on everything—the audience is left pondering these curtain lines:

MAN 1: We just have to trust the Boss.
MAN 2: *(vehemently)* Why?
MAN 1: There's nobody else to trust.

The "bite" may not be in the lines. A piece of stage business may provoke the ending, or a significant action: a hug, a wink, a "twelve pound look," a salute, kneeling to pray, or the slam of a door, as in Ibsen's famous feminist work, *A Doll's House.* Norman Dietz has written a wonderfully oblique Christmas drama, *Deus Ex Machinist,* in which an alienated husband and wife conclude the action with her *touching him* for the very first time in the play.

Using the circularity device to frame your play may be helpful: ending with something that recalls its beginning. We don't need to use the Elizabethan Prologue and Epilogue to do this. My Jonah play, *So Why Does That Weirdo Prophet Keep Watching the Water?* begins and ends on the beach at Nineveh, and the middle is flashback. A readers' theatre piece I wrote, *For All the Saints,* begins and ends with the readers humming that tune. And some of the better one-act playwrights, like Ionesco in *The Bald Soprano* and Millay in *Aria da Capo,* use circularity extensively.

The ending should resolve the action somehow; that is, it should complete the play. But the audience may be left with some unanswered questions, indeed, it *should be* left with them—for example, the "how," the "why," or the "what now?" Mary Hamlin's classic, *He Came Seeing,* concludes with Joab's banishment. This winsome lad, blind from birth but now healed by the Master, is cast out of the synagogue and shunned by his family and friends. We're left with the question, "What now?" Will he follow Jesus? What will happen to him? Such a play may leave the viewers guessing, growing, or groaning for days and weeks later.

This is hard for many of us. As Christians we like to be clear in our witness. So the clash comes between the didactic imperative and the ambiguity that is native to art, the need to preach versus the need for mystery. But the importance of letting people work out their own faith-answers plus the respect we should have for the medium (theatre) requires us often, if not always, to stop short of "spelling it out."

Ergo: Resist the temptation to write plays with sudden, immediate conversions; they may be unbelievable. Conversion is generally gradual, often a long growing process. Nicodemus (John 3:1-21; 7:50-52; and 19:39) was the only person to whom Jesus used the phrase "born again." But Nicodemus, so far as we know, wasn't converted then and there. We find him later arguing for Jesus (John 7:50), but only mildly. So we can assume that Nicodemus' faith was still forming as Jesus died and rose again.

Improvisation and Creation

An improvisation (improv for short) is a relatively spontaneous sketch or role-play without any prepared script. Improvs are used widely for training actors but they can also be used to create a play. Some professional companies, notably Grotowski's "Poor Theatre" and the Becks' "Living Theatre," have used improvs extensively to develop their material.

To invent short plays or stingers, give a word-image like Hope or Faith to small groups of five or six people. They have ten minutes to invent a brief scene and then present it to the entire group. You may specify that their performance be nonverbal, or that it be a tableau, or that it be mime with one punch line; or it can be an improv with regular dialogue.

Or begin with a situation, like a bus stop or two families at the beach. Or assign Bible stories to small groups and ask them to invent parallel situations today and act them out. Or pass out proverbs as the basis for improvs, or Bible fables and fairy-tales, or recent events and anecdotal material. After running the same bit several times you can "fix" characters, brainstorm endings, or just act it out spontaneously until the whole thing seems to "work." Maybe you wind up with a strong dramatic statement!

Everett Robertson, who has used improvs a great deal with Christian actors, argues for the expediency of improvisation: "It is considerably easier to build a play from improvisation than to write one and then learn the lines, stage the action, and rehearse the action for the performance. Improvisation is the most efficient of all dramatic action as far as the use of participant time."[4]

Robertson advises keeping the number of actors small—rarely more than five—and selecting situations involving conflict and unique characters. Keep the scenes short, he says, and work rapidly:

> Avoid long stops between run-throughs of the improvisation. Talk briefly about the improvisations, then perform them. If this process is handled quickly and efficiently without lapses in time and concentration, much more will be achieved in a short period of rehearsal.

It is possible to build a thirty to forty-minute one-act play by improvising episode after episode until you have an entire dramatic sequence.

Using Humor

Where is the human being alive without any sense of humor? Humor is a universal grease that may ease a sticky message past a suspicious audience. Besides that, humor holds attention and binds people together. It is a corporate act; as we laugh together we share something warmly human, intimately personal, almost like *koinonia*. In a superb discussion on "God and Humor," Burbridge and Watts refer to the remark, "'The reason why there aren't more people going into church may well be the looks on the faces of those going out.' Of all people," they write, "Christians should be people who can be happy, who can laugh, enjoy the fun of living, and even laugh at themselves from time to time."[5]

And humor is often educational, even corrective; it exposes human follies and failings. In defending his controversial play, *Tartuffe*, Moliere wrote in his first petition to King Louis XIV:

> The duty of comedy being to correct men's errors in the course of amusing them, I thought there was nothing I could do to greater advantage in the exercise of my profession, than attack the vices of the age by depicting them in ridiculous guise.[6]

So Moliere attacked hypocrisy by making Tartuffe, the hypocrite, the center of his play to "draw attention to the studied posturing of the ultra-godly."

Jesus, too, disliked the ultra-pious—and he had a sense of humor. Otherwise he would not have spoken of a camel going through the eye of a needle or of the beam in your eye (a two-by-four?) that you need to remove before you address the speck in your neighbor's eye! A playwright with a little imagination will take other Bible stories, unhumorous on their surface, and either find or add an appropriate humorous element.

Comic devices. Consider the variety of methods playwrights use to evoke grims or guffaws:

(1) *Incongruity*—any departure from the norm. Man bites dog, elephants fly, children walk backward on a picket fence.

(2) *Surprise*, often coupled with (3) *reversal*. We are amused by the unexpected. The plot takes a strange turn, or someone's fortunes are reversed, or for some reason a character begins singing a different tune.

(4) *Exaggeration*, or *hyperbole*. We have a sense of what is normal, balanced, and proportionate; when something is out of whack, we tend to laugh. Moliere was the master at enlarging a character's basic vice: Sganarelle's selfishness, the miser's greed, the invalid's hypochondria, the hypocrisy of Tartuffe.

(5) *Repetition* often tickles the funny bone. Consider the epic poetry of Daniel 3. We enjoy the litany of repeated instruments (horn, pipe, lyre, trigon, harp, bagpipe, and every kind of music) and officials (the satraps, prefects, governors, and counselors), to say nothing of the refrains: "Worship the golden image that I have set up," and "burning fiery furnace." The repetition resonates: We anticipate each one and it gives the tale a certain rhythm and, eventually, resolution.

Of course, there are nonverbal repetitions as well. Certain stage business or mannerisms may be repeated to provoke guffaws as well as develop character, as the clumsy oaf who keeps tripping over his own feet or the society lady who "sniffs" at people beneath her station.

(6) *Wisecracks* are funny remarks given in response to a situation. In modern comedy, M.A.S.H. abounds in wisecracks with Alan Alda dishing them out like a peanut vendor.

(7) The *pun* is generally a wisecrack involving a bit of wordplay. Words have double (or more) meanings, and this makes our language humorous in itself. Puns can be very obvious or rather

subtle. In *So Why Does That Weirdo Prophet Keep Watching the Water?* I used some obvious puns that worked and more subtle ones that often missed the audience. The storm scene, when Jonah's thrown overboard, ends with three sailors staring at the water quizzically:

> CAPTAIN: (*slowly*) They'll never believe this back home.
> SAILOR 1: No.
> SAILOR 2: But we'll have fun in the telling.
> SAILOR 1: The story of the year. As a matter of fact . . .
> ALL: It's a whale of a tale![7]

Groans, all around.

Later in the belly of the whale, my Jonah meets three odd characters. Adam Smith and Eve Jones are playing cards in the darkness with a mysterious Dealer, who never speaks. Jonah wants to know what brought them there and Eve, referring to the original Garden, tells Jonah, "Now, we would have had the world market, you know, if that fruit had turned out to be Delicious," and Adam interrupts her with, "I think they were Winesaps, dear" (a pun lost on most audiences). Later, Jonah is piqued when somebody interrupts his prayer in the whale's belly. It turns out to be God, who complains, "This experiment with prophets hasn't turned out well so far. . . . Well, if you can't make people turn to me I'll have to send somebody later on who can really do the job. I'll have to get them the word by sending the real Word." (The pun was lost on Jonah, and perhaps the audience too.)

(8) *Confusion* makes us laugh. Pompous doctors try to speak all at once, clowns bump into each other getting through a door, policemen collide chasing a fugitive—all of which can be very close to (9) *slapstick*, although confusion doesn't have to be physical. Slapstick *is* physical, of course: The name derives from ancient comedy when two flat sticks were tied together in such a way that when one character hit another, it would comically double the sound. Today, the pie-in-the-face routine is probably most often identified as slapstick.

Finally, beyond all this—the comic devices, the puns and pratfalls—there is another blessing in humor. It adds a hopeful element to art, strengthening the Divine Comedy. As we laugh at ourselves we can surmount our experience and gain perspective on it. We have an objectivity we lacked before. By laughing at ourselves we gain the courage to overcome that in us which prevents us from growing into the fullness of sons and daughters of God.

Maybe this is part of what the Christian playwright Christopher Fry meant when he said that "laughter is the surest touch of creation in man."

Working with Biblical Materials

Permit me some final thoughts on creating biblically-based drama. In an essay in *Christian Drama* (October, 1981) Earl Reimer asks, "Are Biblical Plays Boring?" The answer is, I think, "sometimes." Reimer contends that when such plays fail to hold the modern audience it may be due to the playwright's having misunderstood the basis for biblical drama, which is *irony*.

As any English teacher knows, there are many kinds of irony. Here one kind concerns us, that irony which you as a viewer feel when you know something the stage characters do not. Classical Greek drama had no suspense; it had irony instead. The audience could pity Oedipus and wince with every new revelation of his roots, for they knew the ending. Irony also functions in biblical drama. We wince as at the last supper Judas asks, "Is it I, Lord?" and we know full well it is he; and we sigh with Caiphas when he says, more wisely than he knows, "It is expedient that one man should die for the people." When the ending (the cross) is foreshadowed by lines and action, we shudder, groan, or grimace— because we know the ending.

Modern playwrights, striving to make their plays original, use suspense as the device for holding the audience. But Reimer is right in saying that irony, not suspense, drives the biblical play because the audience knows the story. Irony can bond an audience as powerfully as suspense, and it tends to move the dramatic event out of the realm of entertainment and into the realm of communion, or *ritual*.

Drama has great power as a connective device. It can help us cross the immense gulf between old Palestine and modern America. It can help us see ourselves in Peter and Judas, and help us find Jesus in our world. I want to suggest four ways of using drama to contemporize scripture, to build bridges between biblical times and the Now. The first is the method most commonly used by writers of biblical plays.

160

Model One. The Biblical Extension Play

Here the writer takes a Bible event or story and extends it by filling in details, adding appropriate characters and dialogue, or in some other way enriching the story. The playwright may choose to develop some often-ignored event or individual, such as the boy who offered his lunch to Jesus for the feeding of the multitude or the young man who ran away naked the night Jesus was arrested. Or the playwright may take the familiar characters and develop them psychologically to an extent where they become, in our minds, "real people" like us and our friends.

Some excellent plays fall into this category, most of them one-acts. Longer biblical plays have seldom been successful commercially. One exception to the rule was *Family Portrait*, a very successful full-length play by Lenore Coffee and William Joyce Cowen that ran on a New York stage in the thirties. The play is unique in that Jesus never appears on stage, but we come to know him well through the eyes of his family and friends, reliving those days of his popularity, rejection, and death. *Family Portrait* is a remarkably beautiful biblical play. Unfortunately, it calls for a sizable cast and is a difficult work for the average church group.

Donald A. Mueller is one of our talented Christian playwrights. His *Eyes Upon the Cross*, similar to the medieval cycle plays, is a series of dramatic vignettes bridged by narration. Each one dramatically enlarges some character or an event, real or imagined, related to the last week of Christ's life.

The action seems to be strictly first century. But Mueller employs a narrator to set up scenes for the audience, make the necessary transitions, and draw theological implications. The boy selling wine, for example, is questioned by the Roman officer who gave the order to crucify Jesus. Eventually the soldier admits that Jesus seemed very different from other criminals he's known—indeed, a unique person, perhaps even—a son of God! The narrator then speaks first to the soldier, then to the audience:

> NARRATOR: So you think he's the Son of God, do you? What difference will that make in your life? Move away, out of the spotlight, off the stage. You have spoken the single line in this drama that gives you immortality. . . . You are changed, that is certain, for you gave the order that crucified him. And we in our pews—we never gave an order that crucified Christ.
> Did we?[8]

Mueller's enacted scenes stay within the biblical frame, keeping it an extension play. But the narrator foreshadows our next category. . . .

Model Two. Mixed-Time Drama

Now we're moving beyond the biblical frame in time and/or location by using creative *anachronism*.

The Greek roots for the word mean, *against time*. So we have an action that's ill-timed, misplaced, or out-of-kilter. Placing hard-hatted construction workers in the mob shouting "Crucify him!" at the trial of Jesus before Pilate—if everyone else was in biblical apparel—would be anachronistic. Anachronism may involve a mixed-time use of language, costuming, stage business, scenery, or even characters. This can be illustrated by having the grim "Doctor" of Auschwitz inspect the fiery "oven" into which Shadrach, Meshach, and Abednego will soon be tossed.

Tebelak and Schwartz, *Godspell*'s writers, used anachronism generously. Events and parables from the gospels are hooks on which the authors hung insightful modern allusions, throbbing contemporary music, and infectious comic routines. The product has upset a few Christians, inspired and uplifted others—but certainly *Godspell* is a mixed-time musical.

In his popular modern Passion Play, *Christ in the Concrete City*, P.W. Turner alternates biblical scenes with contemporary dialogues. He provides his actors with biblical and modern roles. Some of the dialogue is formal free verse; other sections are vernacular, British street talk. In a recent edition he has attempted to Americanize the play but he has only partially succeeded, retaining such British expressions as "king on a flaming donkey" and "multiple store." But the anachronisms are inserted skillfully and they are often humorous; they command our attention and make us ask ourselves, "Is it happening today?" and "Am I very much like James and John and Peter and Judas?" (The play's title makes the main point, of course, and underscores the importance of choosing the Right Title for your play.) The premise is solid. If, as Turner contends, the historical Christ is alive today, we should be able to find him in our world.

M2: Your Galilee, The Galilee of the modern industrial city,
Of the neon lights, and the multiple store.
M4: Where you jostle Christ on the pavement
Among the plate-glass windows.[9]

163

Model Three. The Contemporary Analogue

The extension play stays within the biblical frame; mixed-time drama, while it goes beyond, maintains the Bible as a base to depart from. But if we take a Bible event or story and translate it into a modern setting with twentieth century people and language, and if we seldom or never refer directly to the biblical material in our play, we have more than a mixed-time drama; we have the contemporary analogue.

J.B., Archibald MacLeish's sensitive, thoughtful retelling of the story of Job is such an analogue. Albert Johnson's one-act Job-play, *Whirlwind*, is another example. (Job is Hiram, the owner of a missile-manufacturing plant.) And so is Dorothy Clark Wilson's popular Advent drama, *No Room in the Hotel.*

Ralph Stone's *Construction* is a powerful analogue of the Christ-coming and its implications. The characters are types—representing people we've known—but credible. We can identify. There is a fallen woman, "Dolly," who ironically has more wisdom than most of the assembly. There are two American teenagers, a policeman, a building contractor, a snobbish churchwoman, a minority group member, an exchange student, and a very self-righteous moralist.

164

These people are brought together as strangers, thrown together in limbo, as it were—but, it seems, for a purpose. They discover a heap of building materials in their space along with some tools, and they wonder what they are supposed to be doing. They have heard noises in the darkness beyond their little group, and they are scared, so they set to work building a wall to protect themselves from invaders. When the wall is nearly finished they are surprised by the appearance of a stranger, who calls himself the Builder. He wants them to tear down their precious wall—he claims to know the original blueprints, which call for them to build a bridge instead!

ELIZABETH: Not a wall?
BUILDER: Not a wall, not a wall at all. We have too many of them as it is. We need more bridges—bridges over which traffic can flow both ways, bridges that can take you from here to other places and bring other places to you here.[10]

Obsessed with their fears, they refuse to do as the Builder suggests. Instead, becoming more and more suspicious, they accuse him of being a spy sent by another group. As their rage develops into panic they attack the Builder—they mob and beat him and hang him up to die—during a quick blackout—on a cross they erect from the lumber lying about. When this climax is carefully staged, with a well-timed blackout and then a spot thrown on the cross—or possibly backlighting in red—the audience is left with shock and a sinking feeling. The response is not "What have *they* done?" but rather, "What have *we* done?" Dolly's curtain line is pointed yet unneccessary, in light of what we've experienced: "But we just have to learn; we just have to learn. *We can't go on crucifying the truth forever.*"[11]

Norman Dietz' *Deus Ex Machinist* is more subtle. The title is a play on the Latin, *deus ex machina* (God out of a machine). This is a two-person drama that can be done as readers' theatre. We have a young working-class couple, barely keeping body and soul together in a small flat on Jenkins Street:

HE: Jenkins Street runs in this straight line between Adams n' Saint Pauls.
SHE: It's god's truth.
HE: It runs down beside th' Jenkins Foundry.
SHE: Jis' like an arrow.
HE: It is th' shortes' distance known t' man between McGov-

ern's Mortuary n' this dead end sign at East Water.
SHE: Some distance, wow!
HE: It is what God'n Mister Jenkins made t' git between yester-
 day n' next month's rent. . . .
SHE: There ain't no—whaddyacallum?
HE: Stoplights.[12]

The young couple are tired, short-tempered, impatient with
each other. The plot is simple. They are living hand-to-mouth,
finding it almost impossible to pay their bills, and the wife is
pregnant—the husband is not elated by the fact. Neither is the
wife delighted to discover—she has to wring it out of him—that
he has erupted at work, thrown a crowbar into an engine, and
gotten canned!

There is another story, a mirror-tale told by the wife, of a
young beggar she met at the clinic whose wife, like her, is pregnant. They live in a shack down the street. The beggar is a
carpenter without a job, our best clue that this is an Advent
dialogue. Eventually the wife explains to her husband how she
helped the carpenter's wife have her baby, and this seems to move
him. At the play's end they remain in desperate straits, facing
eviction by their landlady, "Missus Gottlieb," but the dynamic
between them is different somehow. There is an understated yet
hopeful tone.

SHE: That woman just had 'er baby.
HE: Three cheers.
SHE: Yeah. . . . Three cheers. (*There is a silence.*) It's gettin' light
 out. Missus Gottlieb'll be up soon.
HE: Yeah I guess.
SHE: I'll pack things. (*She reaches out and touches him, tenta-
 tively, for the first time in the play.*)[13]

Dietz writes a powerful vernacular poetry, using language to
capture images, evoke feelings. There is a narrative thread, with
refrains that are repeated sagely. But the play is subtle, and many
will fail to see it as an Advent analogue. Most religious drama
tends to err on the side of being too explicit; in several of his plays
Dietz comes close to becoming obscure. But *Deus Ex Machinist*
is a warm and fresh image of Advent, a fine contemporary
analogue.

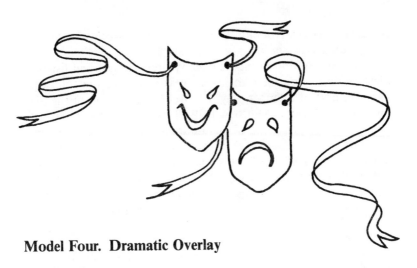

Model Four. Dramatic Overlay

Sometimes called *counterpoint*, dramatic overlay meaningfully combines two or more separate pieces of literature. The result of this hybrid may well be more exciting than the effect of reading or staging each piece separately. We may combine two related poems or two plays, two or more letters, stories or newspaper columns, or any combination of the above. The Bible may be threaded or trellised with essays, plays, poetry, letters to the editor, short stories, or even comic strips.

We have complementary or contrasting overlay, depending on how the materials relate to one another. Suppose you read headlines from the *Times* or the local newspaper while someone else recites the good Samaritan parable, alternating lines; and an acting group mimes the headlines, the Bible story, or both—that's dramatic overlay! If the news story is about a good Samaritan-type deed, like a beggar changing a lady's tire or a Vietnam veteran with disabilities handing out sandwiches to street people, we have supportive or *complementary* overlay. If not, if the story seems ironically to oppose the scripture, we have *contrasting* overlay.

In one class a college student designed a script containing sections of Psalm 136, with the repeated refrain, "For his steadfast love endures forever," juxtaposed against lines from Heller's novel, *Catch-22*. There was sharp contrast: The Heller characters were atheists arguing about what kind of a God they *didn't* believe in, and refusing to be grateful for being born into a messed-up world like this—and yet the psalm is a moving tribute to God and a hymn of gratitude. Staged as a dramatic reading, the

167

contrasting overlay demonstrated the gulf between secular and more sacred views of life.

You seldom find dramatic overlay prepackaged and listed in play catalogs; you have to invent it yourself. In the following passage, part of a longer play, I've trellised a section of the Sermon on the Mount (Matthew 6:19-21) with a husband and wife dialogue. This is a grim, desperate interaction. A young couple stand on the front lawn of their lovely suburban home watching it burn, having saved a few items and lost others. They stand gazing out over the audience, the wife shivering in a blanket. The "Word" would be read from above or behind the audience (perhaps a choir loft, or an invisible voice over a microphone).

THE WORD: Do not lay up for yourselves treasures on earth....
HIM: (*adjusting her blanket*) Are you warmer now? God it's awful!
HER: There goes the trellis! Oh ... (*weeping*) ... Tom, it's our home!
HIM: Thank God the kids are at their grandparents!
THE WORD: ... and where thieves break in and steal ...
HER: How can we tell them? John lost his best clothes in the robbery, and now—
HIM: Rusty's going to miss the stereo mother gave him for Christmas.
THE WORD: ... but lay up for yourselves treasures in heaven ...
HER: What did you say? (*trying to hear*) The fire engines—
HIM: It's noisy as well as cold! I said Rusty's going to be heartbroken. His stereo—
HER: You did save ours, didn't you?
HIM: Hell no, I had my arms full!
HER: Full of those silly three-piece suits—
THE WORD: ... where neither moth nor rust consume and where thieves do not break in and steal ...
HER: To say nothing of that drawer full of Arrow shirts! My word, couldn't you save anything valuable?
THE WORD: ... for where your treasure is, there will your heart be also.

Finally

We've considered four ways of using drama to contemporize the Bible and help find the crossing points between its time and our own. A creative writer, goaded and guided by the Holy Spirit, may produce an imaginative, biblically-based, and truthful play using any of these methods.

Whether you start with the Bible or with modern experience, we need more gifted artists with a Christian vision. Again, not everyone's a gifted playwright. But if you can write, if you like it, and if you have some talent, then write! And if you can't write, then direct, act, or produce good Christian theatre! Genesius will thank you. So will Peter and Paul and the other models whose lives inspire your audiences. And so will the faith-heroes of the ages that your plays affirm and exalt.

New Christians will thank you, those who find Christ in that part of the gospel you enact; and growing Christians too, finding in your characters clues to how to behave as disciples of Christ in a secular world.

And the poor of the world will thank you, the victims of poverty, oppression, greed, pollution, bigotry, violence, and war—if in exposing these evils you provoke reform and give them hope. As you do it "for the least of these" (Matthew 25:45), you do it for Jesus Christ our Lord.

Enjoy Christian theatre!

Notes

Chapter One

1. Benjamin Hunningher, *The Origin of the Theatre*. New York: Hill and Wang, 1961, p. 14.
2. *Ibid.*
3. Harold Ehrensperger, *Religious Drama: Ends and Means*. New York: Abingdon, 1961, p. 77.
4. Stephen M. Archer, *How Theatre Happens*. New York: Macmillan, 1983.
5. Herbert G. May, "Ezekiel," *The Interpreter's Bible*. Nashville: Abingdon, 1956, p. 86.
6. H. M. Kallen, *The Book of Job as a Greek Tragedy Restored*, 1918.
7. Archibald MacLeish, "About a Trespass on a Monument." *New York Times*, Dec. 7, 1959.
8. Murray Roston, *Biblical Drama in England*. Evanston, IL: Northwestern University Press, 1968, p. 319.
9. Archibald MacLeish, *Christian Century*, April 1959, p. 419.
10. Marie Philomene de los Reyes, *The Biblical Theme in Modern Drama*. Quezon City: University of Philippines Press, 1978, p. 70.
11. *Ibid.*, p. 149.
12. For discussion of the Collier controversy, see Joseph Krutch, *Comedy and Conscience After the Restoration*. New York: Columbia University Press, 1924.
13. For an excellent text of Moliere's "Preface to the Edition of 1669," see *Moliere: The Misanthrope and Other Plays* translated by John Wood. Penguin Classics, 1959, p. 101. Copyright © John Wood, 1959. Reproduced by permission of Penguin Books Ltd.
14. Dale Rott, "Drama," in *Christ and the Modern Mind*, Robert Smith, ed. Downers Grove, IL: Intervarsity Press, 1972.
15. Paul Burbridge and Murray Watts, *Time to Act*. Downers Grove, IL: Intervarsity Press, 1979, p. 116.
16. Rott, "Drama," in *Christ and the Modern Mind*, Smith, ed., pp. 41-42.
17. Henry Gheon, "Forward," *The Comedian*. London: Sheed and Ward, 1928.

Chapter Two

1. Elizabeth Burns, *Theatricality: A Study of Convention in the Theatre and in Social Life*. New York: Harper and Row, 1972.

2. Eric Berne, *Games People Play*. New York: Grove Press, 1964.

3. Suzanne K. Langer, *Problems of Art*. New York: Charles Scribner's Sons, 1957, p. 15.

4. Leo Tolstoy, "On Truth in Art," in *What Is Art?* London: Oxford, University Press, 1930.

5. Francis A. Shaeffer, *Art and the Bible*. Downers Grove, IL: Intervarsity Press, 1973, pp. 41, 8.

6. Dorothy Sayers, *The Mind of the Maker*. San Francisco: Harper and Row, 1979, p. 27.

7. Dorothy Sayers, *Begin Here: A War-Time Essay*. London: Victor Gallancz, 1940, p. 23.

8. Clyde S. Kilby, *Christianity and Aesthetics*. Chicago: Intervarsity Press, 1961, p. 10.

9. Sayers, *The Mind of the Maker*, p. 28.

10. *Ibid.*

11. Jacob Bronowski, *Science and Human Values*. New York: Harper and Row, 1972, p. 35.

12. Elizabeth Morgan, "Why Art?" Paper delivered at Eastern College, 1984, pp. 13-14.

13. E. Martin Browne, quoted in Ehrensperger, *Religious Drama*, p. 70.

14. C. S. Lewis, *Of Other Worlds: Essays and Stories*. New York: Harvest/HBJ, 1966, p. 35.

15. Thomas Howard, "Mimesis and Incarnation," in *Imagination and the Spirit*, Charles Hunter, ed. Grand Rapids, MI: Eerdman's, 1971, p. 49.

16. Ernest Ferlita, *The Theatre of Pilgrimage*. New York: Sheed and Ward, 1971.

17. Nancy Tischler, "The Shrinking World of Christian Drama." *Christianity Today*, Oct. 13, 1967.

18. Jerry Gill, "Art and Incarnation" (manuscript), p. 14.

19. See Nelvin Voss, *The Drama of Comedy: Victim and Victor*. Richmond: John Knox, 1966.

20. George Steiner, *The Death of Tragedy*. New York: Alfred A. Knopf, 1961.

21. Christopher Fry, "Comedy," *Adelphi*, Nov. 1950.

Chapter Three

1. E. Martin Browne, Introduction to *Religious Drama 2*. New York: Meridian/Living Age, 1958, p. 7.

2. Oscar G. Brockett, *History of the Theatre*. Boston: Allyn and Bacon, 1970, p. 84.

3. Glynne Wickham, *The Medieval Theatre*. London: St. Martin's Press, 1974, p. 41.

4. Robert Cohen, *Theatre*. Palo Alto, CA: Mayfield, 1981, p. 99.

5. Sarah Longman Payne, "The Crucifixion as Comedy," written at Northern Michigan University, 1976.

6. W. Moelwyn Merchant, *Comedy*. London: Metheun, 1972, p. 35.

7. See the collection, *From Nineveh to Now*. Originally Bethany Press, now available from Gordon Bennett, 1743 Russell Rd., Paoli, PA 19301.

8. Professor George Ralph, Hope College, Holland, MI 49423.

9. Everett Robertson, ed. *Monologues for Church*. Nashville: Convention Press, 1982.

10. See, for example, Iden Payne's *Where Love Is* (Boston: Baker's 1928), or Delores Jaehrling, *Where Love Is, There Is God*, (Colorado Springs: Contemporary Drama Service).

11. Robert L. Short, *The Gospel According to Peanuts*. Richmond: John Knox, 1964.

Chapter Four

1. Kenneth Macgowen, *Footlights Across America*. New York: Harcourt and Brace, 1929, p. 281.

2. Roston, *Biblical Drama in England*, pp. 289-290.

3. *Ibid.*

4. Dorothy Sayers, *The Man Born to Be King*. New York: Harper and Brothers, 1943, p. 6.

5. *Ibid.*, p. 7.

6. Quoted in *Religion and Theatre*, July 1978.

7. Aldersgate Productions, Ltd., 5 Cliff Parade, Penarth, Glen CF6 2BP, United Kingdom.

8. Quotes from *Ride! Ride!* are from *Religion and Theatre*, July 1978.

9. *Religion and Theatre* is edited by Professor Dale Rott, Bethel College, 3900 Bethel Dr., St. Paul, MN 55112.

10. *Christian Drama* is currently edited by Alan Hedges at Malone College, 515 25th St. NW., Canton, OH 44709.

11. Covenant Players, P.O. Box 4001, Woodland Hills, CA 91365.

12. A.D. Players, 2710 W. Alabama, Houston, TX 77098.

13. Lamb's Players, 500 Plaza Blvd., P.O. Box 26, National City, CA 92050.

14. Taproot Theatre Co., 14500 Juanita Dr. NE., Bothell, WA 98011.

15. Jeremiah People, P.O. Box 1984, Thousand Oaks, CA 91860.

16. Iowa Christian Theatre, P.O. Box 322, Washington, IA 52353.

17. Professor M. James Young, Wheaton College, Wheaton, IL 60187.

18. Write Gordon Montgomery, 252 Lakeview Circle, Kingsport, TN 37663, for information.

19. Everett Robertson, ed., *Introduction to Church Drama*. Nashville: Convention Press, 1978.

20. Everett Robertson, ed., *The Ministry of Clowning*. Nashville: Convention Press, 1985.

Chapter Five

1. Olov Hartman, *Three Church Dramas*. Philadelphia: Fortress, 1966, p. viii. Copyright c 1966 by Fortress Press. Used by permission.
2. See Soren Kierkegaard, *Purity of Heart Is to Will One Thing*. New York: Harper Brothers., 1938, p. 181.
3. See William D. Thompson and Gordon C. Bennett, *Dialogue Preaching: The Shared Sermon*. Valley Forge, PA: Judson, 1969.
4. In Norman Dietz, *Fables and Vaudevilles and Plays*. Richmond: John Knox, 1968.
5. From *Church Drama Newsletter*, Church Recreation Dept. (SBC), Jan. 1984.
6. Everett Robertson, ed., *Extra Dimensions in Church Drama*. Nashville: Convention Press, 1977, p. 95.
7. Burbridge and Watts, *Time to Act*.
8. Hartman, *Three Church Dramas*.
9. For additional information: Professor George Ralph, Hope College, Holland, MI 49423.

Chapter Six

1. Gordon C. Bennett, *Readers Theatre Comes to Church*, revised edition. Colorado Springs, Meriwether, 1985.
2. Leslie Irene Coger and Melvin R. White, *Readers Theatre Handbook*. Glenview, IL: Scott, Foresman, 1967, revised 1973, 1982. The first and most comprehensive work on readers theatre.
3. Oscar Rumpf, *Cries from the Hurting Edges of the World*. Richmond: John Knox, 1970.
4. Letter to the author (10/28/85) from Professor Todd Lewis, Biola University, 13800 Biola Ave., La Mirada, CA 90639.

Chapter Seven

1. Carl Allensworth, *The Complete Play Production Handbook*. New York: Harper and Row, 1982.
2. James Hull Miller, *Technical Aspects of Staging in the Church*. Colorado Springs: Contemporary Drama Service.
3. Warren Harris, "On Producing Thornton Wilder's Christmas Play: Problems and Practical Solutions," *Religion and Theatre*, Dec. 1977.
4. Everett Robertson, "Technical Production," *Rec Lab 1981*. Nashville, TN: Church Recreation Dept. Sunday School Board, Southern Baptist Convention, 1981, p. D-63.

5. Jacquie Govier, *Create Your Own Stage Props*. Englewood Cliffs, N.J: Prentice-Hall, 1984.

6. Lucy Barton, *Costuming the Biblical Play*. Boston: Baker's, revised 1962.

7. Judy Gattis Smith, *Drama Through the Church Year*. Colorado Springs: Contemporary Drama Service, 1984.

8. Paul Miller and Dan Dunlap, *Create a Drama Ministry*. Kansas City, MO: Lillenas Publishing Co.

9. Fred Eastman and Louis Wilson, *Drama in the Church*. New York: Samuel French, 1933, pp. 1-2.

Chapter Eight

1. Burbridge and Watts, *Time to Act*, p. 50.

2. *Ibid.*, pp. 52-53.

3. Quotes from *Hark! The Ark!* used by permission of the Lamb's Players.

Chapter Nine

1. Paul T. Nolan, *Writing the One-Act Play for the Amateur Stage*. Cody, WY: Pioneer Drama Service, 1969, pp. 4-5.

2. Nelvin Voss, *The Pendulum of Becoming: Images in Modern Drama*. Grand Rapids, MI: Wm. B. Eerdmans, 1980.

3. Fred Eastman, *Writing the One-Act Religious Play*. New York: Friendship Press, 1948, pp. 56-58

4. Everett Robertson, "Improvisation," in the notebook, *Rec Lab 1981*. Nashville: Church Recreation Dept., Sunday School Board, SBC, 1981, p. D-22.

5. Burbridge and Watts, *Time to Act*, p. 121.

6. Moliere, "First Petition," in *The Misanthrope and Other Plays*, translated by John Wood, p. 104.

7. In Bennett, *From Nineveh to Now*. St. Louis: Bethany Press, 1973, p. 35.

8. Don Mueller, *Eyes Upon the Cross*, p. 37. Copyright by Don A. Mueller, 1959, 1962. Reprinted by permission of Baker's Plays, Boston, MA.

9. P.W. Turner, *Christ in the Concrete City*, pp. 57-58. Copyright by Philip Turner, 1960, 1983. Reprinted by permission of Baker's Plays, Boston, MA.

10. Ralph Stone, *Circus/Parable/Construction*. St. Louis: Bethany Press, 1961, p. 87. Used by permission.

11. *Ibid.*, p. 91.

12. In Dietz, *Fables and Vaudevilles and Plays*, p. 79. Used by permission of the author.

13. *Ibid.*, p. 117.

Resources

Plays Mentioned in the Text

(See also Useful Sources of Material)

Abydos Passion Play, anon.*
Albee, *Zoo Story, The Sand Box*. Dramatists Play Service (DPS).
Anderson, *The Beams Are Creaking*. Baker's Plays (Baker's).
Aristophanes, *The Birds*.*
Auden, *For the Time Being*, in *Religious Drama I*.
Becket, *Waiting for Godot*. DPS.
Bennett, *God Is My Fuehrer*. Friendship Press.
Bennett, *Immediate Delivery*. Contemporary Drama Service. (CDS).
Berryhill, *The Cup of Trembling*. Seabury Press.
Bert, *Woolman*. Write Norman A. Bert, Eastern Montana State College (Theatre Dept.), Billings, MT 59101.
Bolt, *A Man for All Seasons*. Baker's.
Broughton, *The Last Word*. Baker's; also in *Religious Drama III*.
Chapin, *Cotton Patch Gospel*. Dramatic Publishing Co. (DPC).
Clausen, *The Gift and the Glory*. Broadman Press.
Coffee and Cowen, *Family Portrait*. Baker's.
Connelly, *Green Pastures*. DPS.
Coxe and Chapman, *Billy Budd*. DPS; also in *Religious Drama I*.
Crucifixion, The (York cycle), anon.*
Eliot, *Murder in the Cathedral*. Samuel French Inc. (French).
Everyman, anon.*
Gheon, *The Comedian*. Sheed and Ward, London.
Gibson, *The Miracle Worker*. Baker's.
Goodman, *Dust of the Road*. Baker's.
Hamlin, *He Came Seeing*. French.
Hansberry, *A Raisin in the Sun*. Baker's.
Hart and Kaufman, *You Can't Take It with You*. DPS.
Hochhuth, *The Deputy*. French.
Hull, *The Forgotten Man*. DPC.
Ibsen, *An Enemy of the People, A Doll's House*.*
Ionesco, *The Bald Soprano, The Lesson, Exit the King*. Grove Press.
Jaehrling, *Where Love Is, There Is God*. CDS.

Johnson, *Beloved Betrayer, Conquest in Burma, The People Vs. Christ.* Baker's.

Johnson, *Roger Williams and Mary.* Friendship Press.

Johnson, *Whirlwind.* Write Albert Johnson, 33551 Capstan Dr., Launa Niguel, CA 92677.

Kennedy, *The Terrible Meek.* French.

Kopit, *Indians.* Baker's.

Kromer, *For Heaven's Sake* (musical). Baker's.

Kurtz, *A Matter of Death and Life* (somewhat musical). Baker's; *The Holiday*, Baker's.

McFadden, *Why the Chimes Rang.* Baker's.

McFall, *The Case Against Eve.* Baker's.

MacLeish, *J.B.* French.

Mankowitz, *It Should Happen to a Dog.* French; also in *Religious Drama III.*

Masefield, *The Coming of Christ.* Baker's.

Millay, *Aria da Capo.* Baker's.

Miller, *All My Sons, Death of a Salesman.* DPS.

The Miracle of St. Nicholas, anon.*

Moliere, *Tartuffe, The Misanthrope, The Imaginary Invalid.**

Mueller, *Eyes Upon the Cross.* Baker's.

Oberammergau Passion Play, anon.

Odets, *The Flowering Peach.* DPS.

Orwell, *Animal Farm.* Baker's.

Osborne, *Luther.* DPC.

Payne, *Where Love Is* (from Tolstoy). Baker's.

Rice, *The Adding Machine.* French.

Rice and Webber, *Jesus Christ Superstar.* Music Theatre International.

Rutenborn, *The Sign of Jonah.*

Second Shepherd's Play, The (Wakefield cycle), anon.*

Shakespeare, *King Lear, Hamlet, Othello, Macbeth, Merchant of Venice, The Merry Wives of Windsor.**

Shaw, *Man and Superman, St. Joan.* French.

Sheridan, *She Stoops to Conquer.**

Simon, *God's Favorite, The Odd Couple.* Baker's.

Sophocles, *Antigone, Oedipus Rex.**

Stone, *Construction.* Baker's.

Styne, *The Thirteenth Skull* (readers' theatre). Joseph Nichols.

Taylor, *This Is the End.* Baker's.

Tebelak and Schwartz, *Godspell.* Theatre Maximus.

Thomas, *Under Milk Wood.* Baker's.

Thornhill and Thwaites, *Ride! Ride!* Aldersgate Productions. For playbooks and production rights: Ken Osbeck, 107 Ivanhoe NE, Grand Rapids, MI 49506.

Turner, *Christ in the Concrete City, Watch at the World's End.* Baker's.

Wilder, *Our Town, The Skin of Our Teeth, The Long Christmas Dinner, The Happy Journey to Trenton and Camden.* Baker's.

Williams, *A Streetcar Named Desire.* DPS.

Wilson, *No Room in the Hotel.* Baker's.

---

*In public domain. Various sources.

Useful Drama Collections

Barker, Kenneth S., *Dramatic Moments in the Life of Christ* (Atlanta: John Knox, 1978). Seven short biblical plays, with a script copy for each actor/reader.

Bennett, Gordon C., *Happy Tales, Fables, and Plays* (Atlanta: John Knox, 1975). Contains sixteen short readers' theatre pieces, with a tear-sheet copy for each actor/reader.

Bennett, Gordon C., *From Nineveh to Now* (Originally Bethany Press, 1973). Available now from the author at 1743 Russell Rd., Paoli, PA, 19301. Contains three plays based on Old Testament stories, including "So Why Does That Weirdo Prophet Keep Watching the Water?"

Bennett, Gordon C., *Happy Tales, Fables, and Plays* (Atlanta: John Knox, 1975). Contains sixteen short readers theatre pieces, with a tear-sheet copy for each actor/reader.

Burbridge, Paul, and Watts, Murray, *Time to Act* (Downers Grove, IL: Intervarsity, 1979). Contains seventeen dramatic sketches for churches and street theatre.

Brochet, Henri, and Gheon, Henri, *St. Anne and the Gouty Rector* (New York: David McKay). Contains "The Gardener Who Was Afraid of Death," several other plays.

Dietz, Norman, *Fables and Vaudevilles and Plays* (Richmond: John Knox, 1968). Available now from Norman & Sandra, Box 218, Orient, NY 11957.

Habel, Norman, ed, *What Are We Going to Do with All These Rotting Fish?* (Philadelphia: Fortress, 1970). Contains seven other plays as well.

Hartman, Olov, *Three Church Dramas* (Philadelphia: Fortress, 1966). Includes "The Fiery Furnace."

Kurtz, Jack, *Gargoyles, Plastic Balls, and Soup* (Boston: Baker's, 1979). Readers' theatre scripts for Christmas.

Poovey, W. A., *That Wonderful Word Shalom* (Minneapolis: Augsburg, 1975). Dramas on peace. In addition, Poovey has published collections of Lenten and Advent plays, and *Banquets and Beggars,* a collection of plays and meditations on the parables.

Religious Drama I, II, and III. Three paperback collections by Meridian/Living Age Books (New York, 1959). Excellent, hard to find.

Robertson, Everett, ed., *Extra Dimensions in Church Drama* (Nashville: Convention Press (SBC), 1978). Includes a variety of dramatic materials. Also, Robertson has edited collections of *Monologues for Church,* and *Drama in Creative Worship.*

Rogers, Ingrid, *Swords into Plowshares* (Elgin, IL: The Brethren Press, 1983). Large collection on peace and social justice issues.

Rumpf, Oscar, *Cries from the Hurting Edges of the World* (Richmond: John Knox, 1970). Five creative choric readings.

Sayers, Dorothy, *The Man Born to Be King* (New York: Harper and Brothers, 1943). The famous BBC radio series, with notes by the author.

Shaner, Dorcas Diaz, *Short Dramas for the Church* (Valley Forge, PA: Judson, 1980). Mostly monologues and "dramatic duets."

Stone, Ralph, *Circus, Parable, Construction* (St. Louis: Bethany Press, 1961). Now available from Baker's.

Williams, Charles, *Seed of Adam and Other Plays* (London: Oxford University Press, 1948). Contains four modern morality plays.

Useful Sources of Materials

Anchorage Press, P.O. Box 8067, New Orleans, LA 70182. (Primarily children's plays)

Baker's Plays, 100 Chauncey St., Boston, MA 02111.

Broadman Press, 127 Ninth Ave. N., Nashville, TN 37234.

The Coach House Press, Inc., 53 W. Jackson Blvd., Chicago, IL 60604.

Contemporary Drama Service (Meriwether), P.O. Box 7710, Colorado Springs, CO 80933.

Convention Press (Southern Baptist), 127 Ninth Ave. N., Nashville, TN 37234.

The Dramatic Publishing Co., 86 E. Randolph St., Chicago, IL 60601.

Dramatists Play Service, Inc., 440 Park Ave. S., New York, NY 10016.

Friendship Press, P.O. Box 37844, Cincinnati, OH 45237.

Grove Press, Inc., 196 W. Houston St., New York, NY 10014-9983.

Lillenas Publishing Co., P.O. Box 527, Kansas City, MO 64141.

Joseph Nichols Publisher, P.O. Box 2394, Tulsa, OK 74101. (Primarily readers' theatre)

Pioneer Drama Service, 2172 S. Colorado Blvd., Denver, CO 80222.

Readers' Theatre Script Service, P.O. Box 178333, San Diego, CA 92117. (Especially good for children's readers' theatre)

Samuel French, Inc., 25 W. 45th St., New York, NY 10036.

Word, Inc., Box 1790, Waco, TX 76703.

Glossary of Stage Terms

Ad Lib To improvise dialogue spontaneously.

Anchor Weights placed on pieces of scenery or flats to hold them; often sandbags.

Apron That part of the stage projecting beyond the house curtain towards the audience.

Arena Stage space with the audience sitting around it, or on four sides.

Audition To hear candidates reading for roles in a play; also called tryouts.

Backstage Area upstage of the backdrop, where scenery is stored or actors await entrance.

Batten A long three-by-one timber or pipe fastened to the ceiling to provide something from which to hang lighting instruments or drop curtains.

Blackout Cutting all lights suddenly, leaving the stage in total darkness.

Block To plan moves for actors. Blocking refers to the gross stage movement.

Borders Or, border lights, a strip of lights, often covered by gels, generally built in to the proscenium arch or dropped from the ceiling over the stage.

Business Mime or the use of properties by actors on stage.

Cast The actors taking the roles in a play; to select actors for the roles.

Costume Whatever is worn by actors in performances.

Cross A direction for an actor to move from one part of the stage to another, as "Cross left."

Dimout To diminish light slowly, by means of a rheostat or dimmer.

Director The individual responsible for the artistic quality of a production; generally casts the play, runs rehearsals, and decides on staging.

Downstage That part of the stage towards the audience.

Dress Or, dress rehearsal, often the final rehearsal when all actors are in costume and everything is set for performance.

Drop Or, drop curtain or backdrop, a scenic unit that forms a background for the action; may be painted scenery or neutral.

Elipsoidal A spotlight with a sharp-rimmed beam.

Exterior A set representing an outdoor location.

Exit A door in the set or place where actors enter or leave the scene; or a direction to leave the scene.

Flat A rectangular piece of stage scenery made of a wood frame with canvas or another material stretched across it.

Flies Space above the stage area; in a professional theatre, scenery may be "flied" or hung over the stage.

Floor Plan A drawing to scale, showing the position of scenery, furniture, and props in a particular set.

Focus The proper point of attention, either to a dominant actor or a pivotal action, or to a particular line or idea.

Fresnel A common stage lighting instrument, a spotlight producing a soft-rimmed light.

Gel Or, gelatin, a square piece of material fixed in front of a spotlight lens to color the beam of light.

House The audience. Actors speak of a "warm house" or a "cold house" referring to audience feedback.

Improv Or, improvisation, a scene acted out rather spontaneously without benefit of script.

Instrument Generally refers to lighting: any floodlight or spotlight.

Interior A set representing a room or the inside of some building.

Level A stage elevation or riser.

Line Rehearsal A quick "run-through," often without stage movement, to help actors remember/reinforce their lines.

Papier Mâché Paper mixed with glue in proper proportions, for making certain properties or scenery.

Plot The outline of a play's action: what "happens." Also, the arrangement of lighting instruments and sequence of cues for lighting.

Proscenium The "picture frame" of the stage; that is, the front wall through which the audience sees the action.

Quick Study An actor who learns lines early; a "slow study" is one who does not, trying the director's patience.

Scrim A drop curtain made of material that reflects projected images but is transparent when lighted from behind.

Set Stage scenery; or, to put props or scenery in position.

Sight Line A point of vision from any point in the auditorium to any point on stage.

Stage A performance area, whether elevated or not.

Stage Right Or, stage left, positions as seen from actor to audience.

Strike To remove props at the end of a scene; to dismantle a set.

Teaser An adjustable masking border curtain, upstage of the front or "house" curtain.

Tech Run Or, technical rehearsal: rehearsal to set or fix lighting and sound cues or any technical matters.

Top A direction to start the scene from the beginning: "Take it from the top."

Tormentor An adjustable curtain or scenic unit set on the side of the stage to define the width of the acting area.

Trap Or, trapdoor; in professional stages traps may be built into the stage floor for special entrances or effects.

Upstage Towards the back of the stage, or away from the audience.

Warmups Physical exercise to improve fitness and coordination, or simply to "limber up" voice and body just before a rehearsal or performance.

Wings The two sides, just offstage or beyond the set.

Exercises for Actors: Useful Theatre Games

Basic Relaxation Techniques

1. Actors lie on their backs, stretched out on the floor. (A carpet helps). Tell them to relax each muscle group in the body—in sequence from their toes to their head—by tightening the muscles, holding the tension for five seconds, then relaxing. (Take your time with this!) Having moved through the muscle groups in this manner, have them tighten up the entire body, then relax. Breathe deeply. They rise to their feet, slowly, without losing that feeling of relaxed muscular tonus.

2. Have the actors stand relaxed, then shake out their hands and arms until they feel a tingling sensation in their limbs; do the same with the legs. (One at a time!) Unlocking the hips, roll the trunk around on top of the pelvis; unlocking the neck, roll the head around on the shoulders.

Respiration and Voice Projection

1. Have your actors take several deep breaths, then vocalize their breathing: The result is a prolonged grunt. Have them pant like a dog, then vocalize it, grunting sharply. Directing them like a choirmaster, have them quicken or slow the tempo as they grunt, then increase/decrease the loudness. Grunting is excellent for loosening/activating the diaphragm.

2. Give them military commands to work the diaphragm more vigorously, soft on the first part, strong on the command word: "Forword . . . MARCH!" "To the rear . . . MARCH!" etc. (Have them place their hands on their abdomen—they will feel the diaphragm's action on these commands.)

3. For work on breath control, have your actors repeat the alphabet in unison at a steady pace—on one breath. Then have them take a deep breath and count in unison—see how long they can maintain counting. (Whenever they run out of breath they are to stop.)

4. Have them repeat, "One by one we went away," on one breath. Then, in unison, "One by one and two by two we went away," on a single breath. Keep adding to the sentence to challenge your actors to sustain longer breaths, until they have added "ten by ten." Stress the importance of sounding that final consonant on "went" each time through.

5. Pair off your actors and place them at opposite ends of an aisle, or facing walls of an empty room. Taking one pair at a time, have them begin conversing loudly, with strong projection, softening their voices slightly as they walk towards each other; then reverse the process. Then, with pairs facing each other across the room, have one side start talking simultaneously, trying to get a message across to their partners, such as, "What I'm planning for the weekend!' They are to keep talking until the partner raises his/her hand indicating, "I understand." With several pairs a hubbub results, forcing the speakers to use strong voice projection, careful diction, and stronger gestures to be understood.

Articulation, or Diction

1. Have them relax the neck and throat muscles by relaxing the neck and rolling the head around on the shoulders with mouth open and jaw relaxed. If this doesn't relax the jaw, yawn! Then project these sentences, keeping the throat relaxed:
   a. "roll out the barrel"
   b. "slowly go the boats"
   c. "how now brown cow"
   d. "hold the golden moon"
   e. "the cool blue moon"
Once again, half as fast. (Stretch out the vowels!)

2. Sloppy diction results from failing to open the mouth widely and to make full use of the articulators (lips, tongue, teeth, palate) in forming consonants. Say "consonants," feeling the shape of each sound in the mouth (there are seven consonants in "consonants") and be very precise on the final sounds (phonemes) in the word: "consona*nts.*" In unison say (over-enunciating each word): "The tip of the tongue, the lips, and the teeth." Again, faster!

3. Say these lines equally precisely with your actors; then have them increase the speed, retaining that same precision:
   a. "Billy Button bought a bunch of beautiful bananas."
   b. "Peter Piper picked a peck of pickled peppers."
   c. "Truth thrives through thick and thin."
   d. "Wave upon wave of active reservists made a decisive victory."
   e. "Susanna Snooks sings sad, sweet songs."
   f. "The ragged rascal ran around the rugged rock, wretching righteously."
Children's rhymes make excellent choric speaking/diction exercises:
   "Hickory dickory dock,
   The mouse ran up the clock.
   The clock struck one, the mouse ran down,
   Hickory dickory dock."

Concentration and Team-Building

1. Take a short line such as "In the beginning was the Word." In a circle, each actor repeats the line, coming in on the last word of the previous speaker (in this case "Word"), producing an overlap. Try it with longer/shorter lines. Increase the distance between actors and try it. This helps actors play off each other and learn to follow cues more closely (although they will not actually overlap lines on stage.)

2. Sing the song together: "Row, row, row your boat," then sing it again, omitting the last word but going right back to the beginning, without a pause. Keep singing it over, dropping another word off the end each time, resulting finally in everyone's just singing "Row!" try it with other songs for limbering the voice and for concentration.

3. For *visual* concentration, try some nonverbal exercises. First, have them sit in a circle on the floor without talking. The actors are simply to respond physically to the others; the leadership changes as the actors imitate each other's

posture and gestures, nearly moving as a single animal.

    4. Play "follow the leader" with the director appointing someone to lead the line of actors around the room, field, etc. Without talking they follow in each other's footsteps, imitating the previous person. You may call "Reverse!" and the line turns around, or call for an individual to take the lead.

    5. Suggest that anyone may begin working in pantomime on some project (building a snowman, weeding a garden). As others catch on, they silently join the action. When it is completed call "Stop!" and someone else initiates the next action.

Physical Movement

    1. Mirroring: Pair off the actors and have Person B imitate or reflect Person A. Let it go on for a time, then reverse. Coach them to be exact in their mimicry, and to try to anticipate the other's movement so they can virtually become a single unit.

    Create a huge mirror by means of drawing a "line" across the rehearsal space. Still working as pairs but using the entire area, actors will cross each other on either side of the line as those on one side act and those on the other react, or imitate. Coach your actors to be vigorous and imaginative, and to touch others as they interact on their side of the line.

    2. Improvise a scene and play it entirely in nonsense talk or "gibberish," or play it with numbers as lines. This will stimulate vocal and physical expressiveness. Then do an improv in which each actor must find a reason to physically touch every other actor before it is finished.

    3. Have them pantomime a tug-of-war, first with just two players pulling at an imaginary rope, then the whole group divided into teams. Concentrate on giving the rope reality—using as much energy as if it were real.

    4. Create a box-area bounded by invisible walls. Each actor should invent a windup toy (tin soldier, dancing bear, etc.) Using no words but perhaps sounds, the toys begin moving around the box, mechanically, bouncing off walls and one another. Call "Stop," and they freeze.

    5. Create a machine from your actors. Start with one person doing some mechanical motion; in turn, each actor takes a position in line, adding another rhythmic motion, until the machine is formed.

    6. For precision in mime, have them paste a stamp on a letter; open and close a door; pick up and dial a telephone; feed crumbs to the birds; trim a hedge with large clippers; play marbles; balance a stick on their palm; pick up and pet a cat; place a piece of paper in a typewriter, type; etc. These can be varied the second time through by asking each actor to introduce a bit of humor, perhaps an obstacle or frustration, into the action.

    8. Have them form pairs and create team mimes to present; then have them form small groups and create mimes, using Bible stories, historical or recent events; have them invent tableaus—still frames or freezes—to present, with the others guessing what it represents.

Characterization

1. Have them pantomime:
... being happy while playing frisbee
... being sad after breaking their mother's favorite mug
... being tired after working hard on the lawn
... being serene as they watch a sunset
... being sleepy as they head for bed
... being hot and sweaty after a game of tennis ... etc.
2. Have each other walk across the room: "Show by your attitude or by what you're carrying where you're going." ... to bed ... to work ... to the beach ... to a fire ... to a party ... to dinner ... to bowl ... to the grocery store ... etc.
3. With actors forming a large circle around the room, call out persons and attitudes as they walk:
   a. "You're an insurance salesman who's just made his/her first sale!"
   b. "You're a high school student who's been rejected for a date."
   c. "You're the cat that's just eaten the canary!"
   d. "You're a middle-aged high school teacher who can't make a student understand a math problem."
   e. "You're a down-and-out street person grimly prowling an alley for something to eat."
   f. "You're an older person who's been stranded in the wilderness for two days; exhausted and hungry, you spot a town in the distance," etc.
4. Establish a location, such as a bus stop. Ask each actor to invent a character (a wino, a society lady, a high school boy cutting school, a young woman hugging a baby, etc.) and maintain it during the scene. Some interaction should take place. When the bus arrives, all board and the scene's over. Discuss: Who were the characters? How old were they? What did each of them want? Were they consistent? Did the actors really "see" the bus? Did they board it "in character"? etc.

These are a sampling of useful exercises. Most of the good books on acting or voice and articulation contain exercises. Viola Spolin has written the standard volume on theatre games, *Improvisation for the Theatre*, which has recently been abridged and republished under the title, *Theater Games for Rehearsal: A Director's Handbook* (Evanston, IL: Northwestern University Press, 1985). Also, a shorter book is helpful: Fred Owens' *Theatre Games*, which may be secured from Diamond Heights Publishing Co., P.O. Box 14854, San Francisco, CA 94114.

An Actor's Guide to Good Behavior

Some Rules for Behaving Yourself on Stage

1. Always speak louder than you think you need to speak. Be aware of the distance between you and your most distant auditor. Remember, your first obligation to your audience is that you be *heard*. If this is a real problem, ask your director to help you with some voice and breathing exercises.

2. Your second obligation, equally important, is to be *understood*. Speak precisely, and don't slur your words. Again, articulation drills may be helpful.

3. Pick up your cues rapidly; that is, don't leave a "dead space" between the last person's line and your own. Note: This doesn't mean that you need to deliver your lines rapidly—don't rattle them off!

4. Speak from an open position in general, not a closed one.

In Terms of Movement:

5. The action precedes the line (but often just slightly).

6. Make your big movements on your own lines, not someone else's.

7. Cross in front of the actor next to you, not behind him/her.

8. Try to stay visible to the audience; that is, if a downstage actor is blocking you, "cheat" a little.

9. Don't upstage the actor who is prominent at the moment; that is, don't move in such a way as to draw the attention of the audience.

10. Don't just act, but *react*. You need to focus on whomever is speaking (when you are not) and respond physically (facially) to what he or she is saying.

11. Avoid nervous little movements like shuffling your feet. Movement (often called gesture by theatre people) should be *choice* (carefully selected) and *definate* (obvious to the audience, if not to another character). If you're not sure what to do with your hands and feet, do nothing!

12. The cardinal sin for an actor is to *break character*. Don't do it!

13. All of these rules have exceptions to them, even rule #12. (What if there really *is* a fire in the theatre?)

How to Handle Your Director

Check each one that you pass:

_____ I give the rehearsal schedule priority in my life. (Directors hate the line, "I knew we had a rehearsal but . . . .")

_____ Not only do I come, I come to rehearsal on time!

_____ Not only do I come on time, I come prepared! (This means that I know the lines I'm supposed to know. Remember, lines should be learned *at home*—rehearsal time is not for learning lines.)

_____ I try to be coachable. That is, I assume the director knows what he or she is doing, and I try hard to do what is asked of me. (I don't argue with the director—but I am free to raise questions about my character's motivation, to clarify stage business, etc.)

_____ I always take a pencil to the early rehearsals so that I can make notes in my book as the director provides blocking and character suggestions.

Be nice to your director: It's a thankless job. And remember, if your director becomes disgruntled *you* may have to direct the next play! So be coachable, be kind, and be helpful!

187

Darkness and Hope

George Ralph

Hope Reformed Church, Holland, Michigan

I. The Darkness

The Welcome: ("It's a beautiful fall morning, I'm glad you're here—pass it on!")

Call to Worship: God has given us every good gift: the ripened grain, the corn in the field, the squash and the pumpkin on the vine, the apples on the tree.
(Here let the basket of apples be brought in.)
Let us give thanks and celebrate this fruitful season, and rejoice in these bountiful gifts.

Scripture: A river flowed out of Eden to water the garden, and there it divided and became four rivers. The name of the first is Pishon; it is the one which flows around the whole land of Havilah, where there is gold; and the gold of that land is good; bdellium and onyx stone are there. The name of the second river is Gihon; it is the one which flows around the whole land of Cush. And the name of the third river is Hiddekel, which flows east of Assyria. And the fourth river is the Euphrates.

The LORD God took the man and put him in the garden of Eden to till it and keep it (Genesis 2:10-15).

Song: "Morning Has Broken Like the First Morning"

Scripture: And the LORD God commanded the man, saying, "You may freely eat of every tree of the garden; but of the tree of knowledge of good and evil you shall not eat, for in the day that you eat of it you shall surely die" (Genesis 2:16-17).

(Let Eve approach the apples, study them, touch several gingerly. Let her then take one and bite into it. Let her be aware that Adam has come up behind her, and take another apple and give it to him. Adam bites into his also.)

Scripture: So when the woman saw that the tree was good for food, and that it was a delight to the eyes, and that the tree was to be desired to make one wise, she took of its fruit and ate; and she also gave some to her husband, and he ate....And they heard the sound of the LORD God walking in the garden in the cool of the day, and the man and his wife hid themselves from the presence of the LORD God among the trees of the garden (Genesis 3:6, 8).

(Let Adam and Eve here slink away into the congregation; and let those who earlier brought in the apples follow them, carrying the basket. Let Adam and Eve offer apples to the members of the congregation, making certain that everyone takes one; and speaking such lines as "Take a bite," "It's good," "Join us," "Be wise like us," and so forth.)

Scripture:
The LORD God said to the woman,
"I will greatly multiply your pain in childbearing;
    in pain you shall bring forth children,
yet your desire shall be for your husband,
    and he shall rule over you."
And to Adam he said,
"Because you have listened to the voice of your wife,
    and have eaten of the tree
of which I commanded you,
    'You shall not eat of it,'
cursed is the ground because of you;
    in toil you shall eat of it all the days of your life;
thorns and thistles it shall bring forth to you;
    and you shall eat the plants of the field.
In the sweat of your face
    you shall eat bread
till you return to the ground,
    for out of it you were taken;
you are dust,
    and to dust you shall return." (Genesis 3:16-19)

Slides and Music: Violence and destruction in the forces of nature.

Comment: And as man and woman disobeyed God, so man was turned against woman, woman against man, child against parent, beast against beast and beast against humankind; and even nature was turned against man, as man himself tried to force a living from nature, to wrest a blessing from the fruit of his toil.

(Let Abel come forth to place a lamb upon the altar. And let Cain, in his turn, place upon the altar several apples, which he can take from the basket which earlier was placed at the rear of the worship space. Let the two brothers then kneel, with heads bowed, before the altar.)

Scripture: Now Abel was a keeper of sheep, and Cain a tiller of the ground. In the course of time Cain brought to the LORD an offering of the fruit of the ground, and Abel brought of the firstlings of his flock and of their fat portions. And the LORD had regard for Abel and his offering, but for Cain and his offering he had no regard (Genesis 4:2-5).

(Now shall the leader of worship move to the altar and cause the apples to be knocked from the altar onto the ground; let the leader then return to his customary place. He bites from his own apple, and encourages the congregation to do likewise. He will then direct his attention to the scene at the altar. Thereupon let Cain rise, trembling in anger. Let him raise his arm above the kneeling figure of Abel, and bring his hand down violently upon the neck of his brother, causing Abel to collapse upon the ground. Let Cain then pick up from the ground one of the scattered apples—if one of them be within his reach; let him regard the fruit for a moment, and then with it steal away and disappear into the congregation. Abel may remove the lamb from the altar and quietly seek his place among the worshipers after there has begun the reading of the next passage of scripture.)

Scripture: And when they were in the field, Cain rose up against his brother Abel, and killed him. Then the LORD said to Cain, "Where is Abel your brother?" He said, "I do not know; am I my brother's keeper?" And the LORD said, "What have you done? The voice of your brother's blood is crying to me from the ground. And now you are cursed from the ground, which has opened its mouth to receive your brother's blood from your hand. When you till the ground, it shall no longer yield to you its strength; you shall be a fugitive and a wanderer on earth" (Genesis 4:8-12).

Song: "My Lord, What a Morning"

Sentence Prayers of Confession: We have contributed to the wasting of both human and natural resources. Let us confess our sins to Almighty God, our Judge.

(Prayers of confession will end with James Carroll's "Darkness On".)

Song of Assurance of Pardon: "God Gives His People Strength"

II. The Hope

Dialogue and Action:

FIRST LEADER: *(indicating the cross)* The cross is often referred to as "the tree." It was made from wood, from a tree; from part of God's own creation humanity fashioned the instrument on which to put to death God's son.

SECOND LEADER: But the cross is not only a symbol of our sin, our cruelty, our rebellion against God. It also stands for the resurrection which, for the Christian, is the promise of redemption. Even our most wicked acts can be turned by God to good.

FIRST LEADER: *(holding up an apple)* The apple is fruit of another kind of tree. We have been reminded this morning of how this tree symbolizes the possibility that men and women can disobey God; and how this fruit represents all that is terrifying and chaotic and destructive in humanity's and nature's separation from God.

SECOND LEADER: But the seed of the apple can equally well represent the creative power of God, his ability to bring new life out of death. As with the symbol of the cross, we are reminded in the apple seed that God can take the evil we do, and create out of it the means of our salvation.

RESPONDENT 1: Then what is our role? What can we do?

RESPONDENT 2: We can respond to this act of God.

RESPONDENT 3: And this promise of God.

RESPONDENT 4: And this assurance that there is hope for us and for the world of nature.

RESPONDENT 1: Having hope, then, is at least part of what we do.

RESPONDENT 5: Our attitude toward the created order can change too. We can respond to God through our actions, our behavior.

RESPONDENT 3: We can, in a sense, return to the land.

RESPONDENT 2: As Cain fled from the land, after his act of violence.

RESPONDENT 3: We can get in touch again with the rhythms of the earth and nature—the cycle of the seasons—the cycle of planting and harvesting.

RESPONDENT 4: We can plant and we can care for what is growing. We can use nature wisely and tenderly. We can offer praise through our ecology. *(Let the speaker bring what remains of his apple to the foot of the cross.)*

191

RESPONDENT 5: We can reaffirm the value of our work—the toil which is our heritage from Adam. *(Let this speaker bring what remains of his apple to the foot of the cross.)*

RESPONDENT 2: And we can affirm the value of the work of all other people. *(Let this one in like fashion bring his partially eaten apple to the cross.)*

RESPONDENT 3: Our heritage from Eve—the labor of childbirth—can be marveled at again as a miracle of new life. *(And let this one bring his apple core also.)*

RESPONDENT 1: In *all* that we do, whether in relation to the land and nature or in relation to our society, we can perceive that we participate in an act of creation, in the movement of the created order toward full obedience to God. *This last speaker also brings his apple core to the cross.)*

FIRST LEADER: We now invite all of you to bring what remains of your apples to be placed at the foot of the cross—symbolic of both alienation and restoration. The seeds of these apples represent the possibility of new life. From death and destruction God, indeed, can create life and wholeness. Come! *(The congregation will so respond.)*

FIRST LEADER: The apple's fruit and seed undergo decay and tremendous change and strain, in order that the new tree may emerge, come into full strength and flower. So also we decay and strain and tremble, as we yearn for our fulfillment . . . as Paul writes in the eighth chapter of Romans:

SECOND LEADER: Reads Romans 8:18-28, 31 (TEV)

Song: "Joy Is Like the Rain"

Offertory Charge: Let us then, be stewards of our own lives and our own gifts, and stewards of all that God has entrusted to us. As a token of this stewardship, let us bring forth our offerings.
(Let the congregation further be instructed, after they have presented their offerings, to join in a circle around the place of worship.)

Presentation of Offerings

Sentence Prayers of Thanksgiving and Intercession *(Prayers will be followed, as a prayer of supplication, by Michel Quoist's "I Would Like to Rise Very High")*

Charge to the Congregation: Let us consider ways in which we can seek actively to overcome the alienations and antagonisms in our community, in society, and in nature. Let us share aloud, if we will, our suggestions.

Benediction: May God, the giver of hope, fill you with all joy and peace because you trust in him, so that you may have abundant hope through the power of the Holy Spirit. Amen.